# A Man's Guide to a Life Worth Living

*Lessons from Ephesians*

# A Man's Guide to a Life Worth Living

## *Lessons from Ephesians*

Drake McCalister and Mike Sullivan

Emmaus Road Publishing
Steubenville, Ohio
A Division of Catholics United for the Faith
www.emmausroad.org

Emmaus Road Publishing
827 North Fourth Street
Steubenville, Ohio 43952

Library of Congress Control Number: 2014956275
ISBN: 978-1-63446-008-8

Cover design and layout by Alex Renn

# Table of Contents

**Introduction**................................................**vii**
Speaking man-to-man

**1. The Master Plan**.......................................**1**
Seeing your place in the big picture (Eph 1:1–14)

**2. Smart Investing**.......................................**13**
Understanding the importance of understanding your faith (Eph 1:15–23)

**3. Great Comebacks**....................................**25**
You were dead in sin, but made alive through Jesus (Eph 2:1–10)

**4. Strength through Peace**..........................**35**
The power of the Cross brings peace between men and peace between mankind and God (Eph 2:11–22)

**5. Search and Rescue**..................................**45**
Through the Church, God proclaimed the mystery of the Gospel to the world (Eph 3)

**6. Walk Your Talk**.......................................**55**
Live a life worthy of Christ and grow into a mature man (Eph 4:1–16)

**7. An Exercise in Futility**.............................**69**
Without Christ, You will constantly strive and never be satisfied (Eph 4:17–32)

**8. Imitation Is the Sincerest Form of Flattery**..............**81**
Imitate Christ: Walk in the light and not in sin
(Eph 5:1–20)

**9. No Pain, No Gain**........................................................**93**
Christ modeled on the Cross what you are to model for
your wife: sacrifice (Eph 5:21–33)

**10. Lead by Example**.....................................................**105**
Christian manhood in relation to fathers, employees,
and employers (Eph 6:1–9)

**11. Get on Your Knees and Fight Like a Man**.................**115**
How to succeed in your Christian life and in everything
else (Eph 6:10–20)

**12. Finish Well**.............................................................**127**
Fix your eyes on Jesus and run the race together
(Eph 6:21–23)

# Introduction

On a sunny afternoon, a man secretly moves from house to house, but the cover of friendship can no longer offer protection. A once-trusted friend has betrayed him by giving his position to the authorities. His capture is quick, his guilt well known, and immediately he is brought to the courtyard for punishment. Like a recurring nightmare, he receives a sentence of thirty-nine lashes—for this is not his first whipping, but his fifth.

With his hands securely tied, his shirt is ripped from his back and his scar-covered skin is exposed for all to see. The servant of the court firmly grasps the leather handle of the whip and begins to dispense justice. Leather strikes skin. Old wounds reopen. Once again, blood begins to run as he writhes in pain, but he does not plead for mercy.

The man returns to his cell and settles into a familiar pattern of recovery. Years later, reflecting on a lifetime of suffering, he begins to write words that defy human logic, words of encouragement to far-away friends: "I rejoice in my sufferings for your sake, and in my flesh I complete what is lacking in Christ's afflictions for the sake of his body, that is, the Church" (Col 1:24). How is it possible to rejoice in this kind of suffering? How could there be anything redeeming in repeated torture? The minds of most would be thinking of escape, revenge, and crushing the enemy at the first opportunity.

Who would act like this? What kind of man is capable of this level of peace? The man is the Apostle Paul. He arrived at this profound peace, not through his own strength, but through his Lord and Savior Jesus Christ, by the power of the Holy Spirit. Paul discovered the true purpose of life to such an extent that it would have caused him greater suffering to reject Christ and escape torture rather than to profess Christ and endure pain for a brief time.

The Apostle then pens more words of encouragement to another group of friends in the city of Ephesus: "I, Paul, a prisoner for Christ Jesus . . . ask you not to lose heart over what I am suffering for you, which is your glory" (Eph 3:1, 13). Paul endured suffering for the sake of his singular mission: to know Christ and make Him known. He brings to the Church at Ephesus the bold proclamation of the gospel of Christ and his unwavering conviction that Christ is the answer to every question in life—whether about heaven, hell, marriage, sexuality, money, power, career, identity, or anything else.

As the opening dramatization makes clear, Paul speaks to men as a man who has been there. Paul is a man's man. He knew how to take a hit and keep on going. It is likely that he endured more extended suffering than anyone else in Scripture. Aside from receiving thirty-nine lashes five times, he was beaten with rods and shipwrecked three times, and stoned once. Storm-tossed rivers, robbers, Jews, Gentiles, and false friends were frequent threats. Hard labor, hunger, exposure to the cold, and sleeplessness were routine while maintaining oversight of the churches in his care (2 Cor 11:16–33).

Paul does not write like a scholar in his ivory tower or as an observer from the sidelines. He writes from the perspective of someone who has been on the field and in the game, who intimately knows what it takes to live this life. Paul earned the right to speak to men because Christ personally commissioned him, and he lived the gospel he preached.

## An Unlikely Spokesman

Paul, like many of us, is a most unlikely character for God to recruit for His work. Certainly Paul was doing fairly well for himself as a "man of God" before his conversion. He was a Pharisee and a Roman citizen. He had power, authority, credibility, connections; he was a rising star among his peers. Paul, however, was violently anti-Christian. He was commissioned to persecute the young Christian Church and he willingly cast his vote to execute stubborn Christians (Acts 22:4–5, 26:10). During that time, Paul experienced a radical encounter with Jesus.

Visualize what is described in chapter nine of Acts: While on the road to Damascus with the zealous intention to arrest Christians there, Paul, also called Saul, profoundly learns the finiteness of his humanity and the greatness of God. While Scripture is silent on Paul's actual mode of transportation, sacred art almost always depicts him being knocked off his horse on the road to Damascus. He is blinded by a flash of light and falls to ground. Paul then hears these words: "Saul, Saul, why do you persecute me . . . I am Jesus, whom you are persecuting" (Acts 9:4, 5).

Paul realizes that all his power, authority, position, and money are completely insignificant when compared to the living God. Nothing in Paul's earthly authority could match the power of the heavenly reality of Jesus Christ. A simple heavenly flash of light was enough to dethrone and blind Paul. Helplessness marks the beginning of Paul's journey as a servant of Christ, where he exchanges fleeting earthly power and authority for permanent godly power and authority.

## An Invitation

Saul becomes the Apostle Paul, and he is going to speak the Word of God to us through his Letter to the Ephesians. This study is an invitation for you to ponder the truest and deepest things of life, and to gain a power and authority that will stay with you no matter what circumstances life may bring, whether it's unemployment or employment, poverty or riches, obscurity or popularity. Any prize worth having involves work and making commitments. Think of the athlete who achieves his goal with consistent, sacrificial investment—the Christian life is no different.

Like Paul, who was knocked off his horse as he rode with all the earthly authority man could provide, you must ask yourself a question. Am I willing to be knocked off my horse? The horse represents your *pride*, status, safety, and all the earthly things that you think makes life worth living. The horse represents your world of perceived security, but if you are willing to follow the Apostle Paul's lead, you will discover the true life worth living (Ps 20:7).

What do you stand to gain? Everything.

Paul will open up for you the reality that in Jesus Christ you can find your truest purpose in this life and in the next. God created you and everything in this world. Since Jesus is the Author of life (Acts 3:15), when you live life by His standards and with His understanding, the Christian life becomes so powerfully appealing that any alternatives are not worth your time. It would be like choosing to play a football video game rather than a starting position in the Super Bowl.

What do you stand to lose? Everything.

Well, everything of worldly, fleeting value in exchange for the eternal, enduring riches of Christ that *truly* make life worth living. We are not talking about gaining abstract benefits, but the very keys to success and satisfaction in the essentials of life: marriage, family, business, sexuality, money, friendships, and most importantly, getting to heaven. This is not to say that following Christ is easy, and the Apostle Paul makes that clear through his suffering.

## The Importance of Bible Study

Nearly sixteen hundred years ago St. Jerome penned the words, "Ignorance of the Scriptures is ignorance of Christ."[1] This is a bold

---

1. See Vatican II, Dogmatic Constitution On Divine Revelation *Dei Verbum*

statement and the Catholic Church has taken these words and made them her own. The Church seeks to remind the faithful that there is no substitute for knowing Scripture; if you ignore Scripture, you risk not truly knowing Christ.

This Bible study will take you through the New Testament's Letter of Paul to the Ephesians. The Apostle Paul wrote this letter to the Church in the growing metropolis of Ephesus, and it most likely circulated throughout the surrounding cities. This letter is short, easy to read, and packed with wisdom and knowledge that is profound and practical in every way. As you go through this study, you will find power in God's Word; the more you soak in Scripture, the more practical it becomes. Ephesians enables you to grow in your knowledge of Christ and the Christian life as well as that of the Apostle Paul.

Paul gave everything to God so that you and countless others could hear the saving gospel of Jesus Christ. How did Paul feel about losing everything, but gaining Christ? He says: "Indeed I count everything as loss because of the surpassing worth of knowing Christ Jesus my Lord. For his sake I have suffered the loss of all things, and count them as refuse, in order that I may gain Christ and be found in Him" (Phil 3:8–9). Paul knows that nothing, absolutely nothing, compares to truly knowing Jesus Christ. Once you know Jesus, you will never want to return to your former life. Paul invites us to grow up into "mature manhood" in our physical and spiritual life as we come to know the "fullness of Christ" (Eph 4:13).

Paul has this confidence because he knows that life's goal is to prepare for eternal life with God in heaven (CCC 1024, Mt 25). As you learn the fundamentals of the Christian life, you will grow in holiness (Heb 12:14), which will prepare you for heaven. That is the value of a Bible study. A mature man in everyday life is one who physically provides for and protects his family, and the world is full of men who leave this responsibility to others. To be a mature man in your spiritual life means that you must *spiritually* provide for and *spiritually* protect yourself and your family. Do not leave this task to

(November 18, 1965), 25; CCC 133.

someone else, because God will hold you eternally accountable for your actions in this life (Mt 25.31–46).

We do not follow Jesus simply as life's coping mechanism. We follow Jesus because it is a matter of eternal life. As Paul says to the Corinthians, "If for this life only we have hoped in Christ, we are of all men most to be pitied" (1Cor 15:19). As you come into deeper relationship with Jesus through the teaching of Paul, you will find more success in this life—you will find a life worth living—and will be better prepared for eternal life.

## How to Use This Bible Study

You can do this Bible study alone or with a group of men. The word "study" in "Bible study" can be misleading. You will certainly grow in knowledge, but the chief goal in studying the Bible is to know Jesus Christ. It is crucial not to view your study as an academic exercise. This is practical, and the first practical act that should accompany all Bible study is prayer. When combining prayer with studying Scripture, an exchange takes place. Through prayer we speak to God; through Scripture He speaks to us—a conversation between God and man (see CCC 2653).

Furthermore, your success rests on your familiarity with the Letter to Ephesians. Read Ephesians several times throughout the study. Don't worry; the whole letter is only about four pages long. Reading should be prayerful and reflective. The more you read it, the more you will understand. Eventually, by the end of this study, you should have a genuine understanding of Ephesians. At the same time, if you follow the outline below, you will see a marked difference in your life.

Below is a recommended pattern of prayer and reading as you work through this Bible study.

Pray Monday–Friday (30 seconds minimum and more if you can)

Ask God to open your heart and mind to the Scriptures. Your prayer could be as simple as this:

In the name of the Father and of the Son
and of the Holy Spirit.
Heavenly Father, open my heart and mind
to Your Scriptures. Jesus, forgive my sins of
thought, word, and deed so that nothing will
stand between me and You. Holy Spirit, show
me the truth and help me see where
You want me to change.
Amen.

If you have time, also pray a decade of the Rosary or a full Rosary. The bottom line is that there is no such thing as too much prayer. Prayer is like investing in your retirement account: the more you put in now, the more you will receive later.

Read Ephesians Monday–Friday (10 minutes minimum and more if you can).

Read a little of Ephesians every day so that it slowly becomes a part of you. The best way is to read and then take some time to think about the reading, asking God to help you understand.

Monday:Read chapters one and two
Tuesday:Read chapter three
Wednesday:Read chapter four
Thursday:Read chapter five
Friday:Read chapter six

Read One Chapter a Week of this Bible Study.

Finally, read one chapter a week in this book and answer the questions. The goal of this study is not to finish, but to allow the truth of God's Word to draw you closer to Jesus Christ and transform your actions. This means the study proceeds slowly. Each chapter in this Bible study covers about half a chapter from Ephesians. Reading in this manner will allow you to reflect throughout the week on the reading, the questions, and how both relate to your life.

Be prepared for God to meet you and transform you as you

read the Bible and apply it to your life. God promises that if we are faithful to seek Him first, the rest of life will fall into place (Mt 6:33). Give God a chance to make good on His promise. You will not be disappointed. You may be challenged and stretched, but not disappointed. He will not be outdone in generosity!

May you be blessed by this study and may God give you the grace to grow into mature manhood and discover a life truly worth living.

# CHAPTER 1

# The Master Plan

Seeing your place in the big picture
EPHESIANS 1:1–14

The year is 1969. The plan is straightforward: launch a manned spacecraft from Earth, land on the moon, and come home. Like any good plan, the basic goal is clear but the actual implementation requires overcoming a series of monumental obstacles.

The first and most obvious obstacle is Earth's gravity. To escape its pull, a 360-foot Saturn V rocket is constructed with 350,000 gallons of rocket fuel, serving 7 million pounds of thrust (roughly 150 times more powerful than an average fighter jet) with an acceleration of zero to 17,000 miles per hour in about 12 minutes.

Three men are seated in the command module atop the rocket. The ignition sequence commences, then liftoff. First, altitude is needed, then acceleration. In just under 12 minutes the astronauts are in orbit.

The command module flies for 8 days, reaching a maximum speed of 25,000 miles per hour, before slowing as it approaches the moon. The module must fly close enough to the moon to be caught in its gravity, slingshot around, enter into orbit, and eventually land. There is only one shot at this. The command module cannot make major course changes, but only adjustments. The margin of error for this master plan was determined by engineers at NASA long before the launch. Fly too close to the moon and the astronauts will crash. Fly too far from the moon and they will miss the moon.

Once in the moon's orbit, the lunar module separates and astronauts prepare for landing. As the module descends, they still have no idea if the dust on the surface is six inches or two feet deep. Anticipation builds as landing thrusters fire. They land safely, exhaling a big sigh of relief. Neil Armstrong exits the lunar module and is the first man to walk on the moon.

The moon is the most hostile environment any human has ever encountered. There is no atmosphere. Space is silent. There is no sound other than radio communication, accelerated heartbeats, and the well-paced breathing of the astronauts. Temperatures can range from more than 200 degrees Fahrenheit in the sunlight to less than minus 200 in the shade. Engineering a space suit to endure this environment is no small feat.

Once the mission on the moon is completed and the lunar module safely docked, the main engine of the command module is fired to escape the moon's gravity and head toward Earth. This last stage is the most crucial and poses the greatest risk of the voyage.

As the module approaches Earth, there are three possible angles of reentry into the Earth's atmosphere, two of which are deadly. If the approach is too shallow, the module will skip off the atmosphere like a rock skipping off water in a pond. If the approach is too steep, the module will descend too quickly and burn from the friction. The angle that NASA engineers think will return the module and men safely is minus 6.5 degrees, with less than 1 degree margin for error.

Once they enter into the Earth's atmosphere, the course is set; there is no return and there is no adjustment.

The command module enters the atmosphere. The roar of oxygen enveloping the capsule replaces the silence of space. The exterior of the module heats to nearly 2,000 degrees. The men race to earth at 20,000 miles per hour, gradually slowed by the atmosphere. The parachutes deploy, and the module slowly descends to earth and gently splashes down in the ocean.

Mission accomplished!

The depth and detail of the master plan needed to go successfully to the moon and back could fill several volumes. Millions of man-hours and billions of dollars were expended for a brief two-year project. When surveying this achievement of man, it is appropriate to be in awe and impressed with the scope and success of the mission.

## The Master of All Plans | Verses 9–10

"FOR HE HAS MADE KNOWN TO US IN ALL WISDOM AND INSIGHT THE MYSTERY OF HIS WILL, ACCORDING TO HIS PURPOSE WHICH HE SET FORTH IN CHRIST AS A PLAN FOR THE FULLNESS OF TIME, TO UNITE ALL THINGS IN HIM, THINGS IN HEAVEN AND THINGS ON EARTH."

Just like the Apollo moon landing, God has a detailed master plan for all of humanity, including you. In these opening verses of Ephesians, Paul reveals that God has been orchestrating a divine master plan and has ordered all of human history so that you could know Him personally. The complexity and depth of *this* plan makes the Apollo moon-landing mere child's play. God's plan is complex, not in a confusing way, but *mysterious* and situated as it is outside of time. We are incapable of knowing or grasping God's plan and are required to "walk by faith, not by sight" and trusting that "all things work to the good for those who have faith." God's plan is so profoundly complete that every person who has ever lived is allowed to know Him personally. Everyone is included in God's plan, whether they know it or not, acknowledge it or not, desire it or not, for God is the God of all and the Author of all.

The Apollo mission was designed to get one rocket to one location and back. God's master plan is simultaneously directing six billion people from conception to eternity, as well as all those who lived before and those who will come later.

Paul tells us that, in Christ, God has revealed the details of this master plan at just the right time (Eph 1:9–10). What is the ultimate goal of this plan? To "unite all things" to Christ.

## The Big Picture

There is a philosophical way of looking at what it means to be human. Some things, such as human nature and dignity, are essential. That is to say, they are present in *every* person without exception and are inviolable: They cannot, under any circumstances, be forfeited or taken away. As difficult as this may seem, even someone like Hitler, Stalin, or a child molester, despite the horrors they have committed, cannot be treated in such a way as to reduce them to something less than human. In short, we cannot, and must not, do unto them even as they have done unto others. Other things, such as particular qualities (eye color, level of intelligence) and voluntary actions (reading, working) are accidental or contingent. They are subject to change and dependent on or determined by another cause.

What gives your life purpose? What gives your life meaning? Is it external things like your job, wealth, or respect? Is it qualities like your physique, mind, or personality? Any value in life that comes from accidental things can always be taken away. This does not mean that they are bad. In fact they can be quite good. But if your main reason for living is rooted in a non-essential good, what happens when that is taken away? Let's face it. Jobs are lost. Bodies get old. Loved ones die.

The greatest peace and security in life comes in realizing that you have personal worth and value because the One who created all things created you. Once you grab hold of this reality, your life will never be the same. Paul discovered this, and in his Letter to the Philippians he says that he has learned to be content, whether blessed with wealth or poverty, and that through Christ he can accomplish whatever lies before him (Phil 4:11–13). This perspective is essential for understanding the big picture.

Have you ever looked at a close-up of a high resolution picture? You can see great detail, but are unable to see the complete picture. If you only view it up close you will become frustrated, unable to see what the photographer intended. Paul lays out for us in these opening verses of Ephesians the big picture of God's master plan.

Step back and take in the view.

## Master Plan Highlights

### Heaven | Verse 3

"**Blessed be the God and Father of our Lord Jesus Christ, who has blessed us in Christ with every spiritual blessing in the heavenly places.**"

First, notice that Paul orients us toward our true home and ultimate goal: heaven. If you have freely responded to Christ through faith and baptism, you are *in* Christ and a member of God's household (Eph 2:19). Paul tells us that we have every spiritual blessing in the heavenly places (verse 3). What does this mean? God has not withheld anything from you. You do not need to beg God as if He were a miserly banker unwilling to part with His money. You are able to approach God to receive the powerful blessings He has already given (see also Heb 4:14–16). These blessings begin in this life and come to completion in heaven.

### Chosen | Verses 3–4

"**Blessed be the God and Father of our Lord Jesus Christ, who has blessed us in Christ with every spiritual blessing in the heavenly places, even as he chose us in him before the foundation of the world, that we should be holy and blameless before him.**"

Heaven is our home and we are made for heaven. Paul reminds us that we are not products of random chance, but that God personally chose each of us—before time began (verse 4). You are not the result of an evolutionary accident; you are a unique creation made in the image and likeness of God. You have purpose and value because the Creator of matter says *you* matter.

## God loves *you* | Verse 5

**"HE DESTINED US IN LOVE TO BE HIS SONS THROUGH JESUS
CHRIST, ACCORDING TO THE PURPOSE OF HIS WILL."**

Even while knowing that He created us, it is easy to view God
as the great cop in the sky, just waiting to catch people sinning with
His holy radar gun. Some may even feel that God derives pleasure
from our punishment or suffering. Paul sets the record straight and
teaches us that God designed this entire plan out of His great love
for us, and the Apostle John tells us that God *is* love (1 Jn 4:7–8,
16). God does not try to love or to put on love. He *is* pure love. He
can be nothing other. True love will always desire the other person's
highest good. Therefore, God will naturally always do what is best
for us. We, on the other hand, have to learn how to love and how to
accept love. Our ability to receive or give love depends on connecting
with the One who *is* love.

## Sons | Verses 5–6

**"HE DESTINED US IN LOVE TO BE HIS SONS THROUGH JESUS
CHRIST, ACCORDING TO THE PURPOSE OF HIS WILL, TO THE PRAISE
OF HIS GLORIOUS GRACE WHICH HE FREELY BESTOWED ON US
IN THE BELOVED."**

The next phrase is packed with cultural meaning, easily
understood by a first-century reader but largely lost on a twenty-
first-century reader. Paul says that we are destined to be sons
through Jesus Christ (verse 5). We are destined to be not only
sons, but also first-born sons (Gal 3:26–4:7; Heb 12:22–23). In
Hebrew culture, a first-born son received a special blessing and the
fullness of his father's inheritance and authority (Gen 27). Within
the nation of Israel, God originally intended the first-born males
to have a priestly role of service to Him (Ex 13:11–16, Lev 3). In
most kingdoms, the first-born son is the successor to the throne
and therefore to the kingdom.

Jesus is the true first-born Son through whom we now receive our adoption as sons (Rom 8:23, 29; Col 1:15). If you are a Christian man, this is your true identity: You are a first-born son of the King endowed—by virtue of your baptism—with the fullness of His blessing and inheritance. (The meaning of this applies to men and women.) Through faith and Baptism, you have become true co-heirs with Christ to God's kingdom (CCC 1265). It is worth quoting a few verses from Paul's Letter to the Romans to drive this point home.

> For all who are led by the Spirit of God are sons of God. For you did not receive the spirit of slavery to fall back into fear, but you have received the spirit of sonship. When we cry, "Abba! Father!" it is the Spirit himself bearing witness with our spirit that we are children of God, and if children, then heirs, heirs of God and fellow heirs with Christ, provided we suffer with him in order that we may also be glorified with him. (Rom 8:14–17)

You do not have to settle for handouts and leftovers. You are able to approach God as a son whom He desires to bless. This does not mean God will give you whatever you request, but He will always do what is best for you when you ask. God is a perfect, loving Father.

## Redemption | Verses 7–8

**"IN HIM WE HAVE REDEMPTION THROUGH HIS BLOOD, THE FORGIVENESS OF OUR TRESPASSES, ACCORDING TO THE RICHES OF HIS GRACE WHICH HE LAVISHED UPON US."**

If we are honest, it does not take much reflection to realize and admit that we sin. Most men have struggled with any number of issues: anger, lust, pride, selfishness, greed, and the abuse of food, alcohol, tobacco, or drugs. This is not new information and it is no surprise. Men have been struggling with these issues since the beginning (Gen 3). Our sin separates us from God because God is perfect and no sin can dwell with Him. As long as we are enslaved by sin, we are separated from God.

The good news of the Gospel is that, in love, the Father sent His Son Jesus to *conquer* sin and death, redeem us, and forgive us through a gratuitous gift of His grace (see Rom 5:8).. Once we committed an actual sin, we became personally guilty and received the full penalty for sin (Rom 6:23). Since God is supernatural (above the natural) and we are natural, we could not repair the breach between God and us on our own. Only God could repair this breach. The natural cannot reach the supernatural on its own. Without Christ and the Cross, we are stuck with the proverbial "can't get there from here" in relation to our desire for heaven.

It is often said that Jesus paid a debt He did not owe, because we owed a debt we could not pay. The profound good news of God's forgiveness cannot be overstated. No matter what you have done, God can, will, and desires to forgive you. No matter how many times you bring your sins to a priest in Confession, Jesus will always forgive you, as long as you are truly sorry. Like the father in the parable of the prodigal son (Lk 15:11–32), God the Father stands ever-ready to forgive you and restore you to your rightful inheritance. Going to Confession should be one of the greatest experiences for Catholics and should always bring a smile to one's face. What could be better than the lavish grace of God's forgiveness?

## Appointed to Live | Verses 11-12

**"IN HIM, ACCORDING TO THE PURPOSE OF HIM WHO ACCOMPLISHES ALL THINGS ACCORDING TO THE COUNSEL OF HIS WILL, WE WHO FIRST HOPED IN CHRIST HAVE BEEN DESTINED AND APPOINTED TO LIVE FOR THE PRAISE OF HIS GLORY."**

Why should you invest time into your Christian faith? Because Christ is the key to everything in this life and the next. Paul reminds us that it is God, not us, who accomplishes all things in our Christian walk. We cannot overcome this world by our own strength, but only by the power of the Holy Spirit. Paul also tells us that God will do all things according to His will. This means that we might not always understand God's plan, but we can always be sure that His plan is the best.

Our relationship to God can often be like that of a son to his father. A father may tell his three-year-old son not to run into the street. The saving truth of this information does not depend upon the child's understanding, but lies in the obedience of the child. As the child grows, he will come to see the wisdom that the father knew all along. This is much the same with God and us.

Ultimately, God is accomplishing His will in us because we are appointed to live. We were not meant to simply survive, but to thrive (Jn 10:10). To thrive does not depend on material possessions. Rather, it depends on a spiritual deposit that comes through faith in Jesus Christ and obedience to His will. God desires us to live for His glory, not ours.

## Guarantee | Verses 13–14

"IN HIM YOU ALSO, WHO HAVE HEARD THE WORD OF TRUTH, THE GOSPEL OF YOUR SALVATION, AND HAVE BELIEVED IN HIM, WERE SEALED WITH THE PROMISED HOLY SPIRIT, WHO IS THE GUARANTEE OF OUR INHERITANCE UNTIL WE ACQUIRE POSSESSION OF IT, TO THE PRAISE OF HIS GLORY."

Finally, Paul teaches us that, just like a man who puts down a deposit guaranteeing his purchase of a product, God has given us the Holy Spirit guaranteeing our coming heavenly inheritance to those who have believed the Gospel. You first receive the Holy Spirit in Baptism, and Confirmation completes the deposit of the Holy Spirit. The Holy Spirit is given to us to be our power outlet to God, which allows us to live the Christian life effectively. We must realize and accept the reality that we cannot follow Christ on our own strength, but only by the power of God through the Holy Spirit (Gal 5:16–18). Jesus told the Apostles they would receive power through the Holy Spirit (Acts 1:8). Every baptized and confirmed person has this power and must cultivate it. The Holy Spirit is the active agent who allows us to overcome sin and temptation and empowers us to live for God.

## Conclusion

Before time began, God laid out an intricate master plan so that you could know Him personally and live the fullest life possible in this life and the next. What is the big picture? You are *not* an accident. God has chosen *you* in love to be His son and a full heir to His kingdom. Even though you sin, Jesus has redeemed you and forgiven you through the Cross. All of this is so that you can live a powerful life by the Spirit of God.

Do not settle for second best. You are a son of the King and He has given you everything you need. Call on Him and He will answer. And when you do, you will want to shout

I am no longer defined
By all the wreckage behind
The one who makes all things new
Has proven it's true
Just take a look at my life

Hello, my name is child of the one true King[1]

---

1. Matthew West is a Christian Contemporary-Pop-Rock musician. "Hello My Name Is" is the second No. 1 song from his October 2012 GRAMMY-nominated album "Into The Light." It was released on September 25, 2012 through Sparrow Records.

## Study Questions

1. What things make it hard to believe that God has a master plan for your life?

2. What areas of your life do you tend to reserve for your own leadership, unwilling to surrender them to God?

3. When you step back and look at the bigger picture of your life through God's eyes, do some things become clearer? Do they begin to make sense? In what ways?

4. If God is not the great cop in the sky, how do you describe Him?

5. Do you sometimes feel you are only getting handouts and leftovers from God? Explain.

6. What is an example of something you have tried to overcome with your own strength that you would now like God to help you with?

7. God means for you to thrive, not just survive. Can you thrive when you fail? Can you thrive when you lose a job? Can you thrive when you are rejected? List some examples.

# CHAPTER 2

# Smart Investing

---

Understanding the importance of understanding your faith
EPHESIANS 1:15–23

It may be hard to remember, but there actually was a time when the word "dot-com" meant nothing. Not many years ago, if you said "Amazon" or "Google" in public, you would be greeted by blank stares. These words have now become a part of the American popular lexicon, with "Google" being officially added to the dictionary in 2006.

The 1990s were a time of unparalleled growth in technology. Not only were tech companies growing, but their stock prices rose at an unprecedented rate. The time was right, or so it seemed, for anybody and everybody to get into the dot-com business, and get in they did. Almost overnight the expectation emerged that all one needed was a website, and suddenly the world was his market place. The new gold rush was on to see who could stake his claim and become rich.

By 2000, ever-rising stock prices, market confidence, and huge amounts of available venture capital created a novel "get-big-fast" business model, and the showcase for it was Super Bowl XXXIV. Seventeen dot-com companies paid millions of dollars in hopes of having a thirty-second ad emblazon their dot-com name in the minds and pocketbooks of viewers. One company in particular became the poster-child for this dot-com revolution: Pets.com.

Pets.com started in 1998 and believed they could fill a niche by selling pet supplies online. They began to successfully expand and establish their business via an innovative marketing campaign featuring a sock puppet dog. As Super Bowl XXXIV neared, Pets.com decided to go for broke and invest over one million dollars in a creative ad. The commercial was a runaway success. It was ranked as the number one ad in many polls, as well as the most memorable of all Super Bowl commercials.

So how did Pets.com do? The company went public in February 2000 (one month after the Super Bowl) with an opening stock price of over eleven dollars. Nine months later, the company was liquidated (closed) with a stock price of nineteen cents. That's right, in nine months the company went from king-of-the-hill to crap-in-the-can. Pets.com had a great idea, but they did not employ proven, traditional methods of growth and investment. This caused an excessive imbalance in their income to debt ratio and their revenue stream could not grow fast enough to cover expenses. The results were disastrous.

Pets.com was the last dot-com company to go public before the dot-com bubble burst. Companies that year closed as fast as they opened. Jobs were lost, dreams were shattered, and stocks fell like meteors from space. The next year, when Super Bowl XXXV aired, only three dot-coms ran ads.

Many people lost their shirts by not following sound investment principles during the rise of the dot-coms. Companies like Amazon and Google followed tried-and-true strategies of slow, consistent growth, which allowed them to survive the dot-com bust and become formidable forces in the global market place. The secret to smart investing is not in getting lucky, but in making clear, well-informed, well-thought-out decisions.

### Investing to Win

Any financial investment is made with an expectation of gain. The success of an investment rests on knowledge of the market and on sound investment strategies. To give your money without knowledge of where it is going or who will be investing it calls to mind the old proverb, "a fool and his money are soon parted."

Our Christian faith is much the same. There is a way to make good spiritual investments that will yield great returns and there is a way to quickly lose what little you have. The key is understanding the Christian faith. Not simply an academic understanding, but an intimate understanding deposited by God the Father, rooted in the work of Jesus Christ, and fueled by the power of the Holy Spirit.

As Paul makes clear throughout his letter, understanding the spiritual life is the key to understanding the physical life. Things like work, money, recreation, friends, family, marriage, and sexuality are all given to us by God. The more we get to know God, the greater success and satisfaction we can have in every area of life. Christ is the key to everything in this life and the next.

## Paul's Prayer for Understanding

This next section begins with Paul's powerful prayer asking God to increase the understanding of the Christian faith in the Church at Ephesus. The more you understand your Christian faith, the more Jesus Christ will transform you. This prayer is one you can take and make your own.

## Thankfulness | Verse 16

**"I DO NOT CEASE TO GIVE THANKS FOR YOU, REMEMBERING YOU IN MY PRAYERS."**

Paul starts his prayer by giving thanks. Thankfulness is a non-negotiable aspect of the Christian life. When thankfulness is lacking, understanding becomes impossible. Paul writes to the Church at Philippi, "Have no anxiety about anything, but in everything by prayer and supplication with thanksgiving let your requests be made known to God" (Phil 4:6). Being thankful means taking time to recognize the blessings you have already received.

If you have children or have worked with children, you know

how a little ingratitude can ruin a perfectly good day. You might have taken the kids to the park, played games, and bought them ice cream. As a dad, at least for this day you're thinking you're doing pretty well. But leaving the ice cream shop, cones in hand, you hear, "His ice cream is bigger than mine." And then, "That's because I'm better than you." Within moments, the perfect day spirals into a showcase of ingratitude. The kids are fighting, you find yourself yelling, and when you arrive home your wife gives you the "what did you do" look.

With a little honest examination we can admit we often do the same thing to God. After all that God has provided for us—food, clothes, shelter, and, above all, sending His Son to die for us—we can find ourselves being unthankful for the blessings we have received or comparing our blessings to another's.

Thankfulness is so important that we have a sacrament named after it: Eucharist. "Eucharist" is a Greek word meaning "thanksgiving."[1] Every time we go to Mass the high point of the liturgy is when we "give thanks" (Eucharist) for the saving sacrifice of Jesus Christ on the Cross.

### Growing in the Knowledge of God | Verse 17

**"THAT THE GOD OF OUR LORD JESUS CHRIST, THE FATHER OF GLORY, MAY GIVE YOU A SPIRIT OF WISDOM AND OF REVELATION IN THE KNOWLEDGE OF HIM."**

Paul prays for two things to help us grow in the knowledge of God: wisdom and revelation. What makes the difference between a good decision and a bad decision? Wisdom. If you are wise, you possess the necessary understanding to make good decisions. Scripture is filled with exhortations to grow in wisdom. Here are two prominent passages from Proverbs:

> Trust in the LORD with all your heart, and do
> not rely on your own insight. In all your ways

---

1. See Lk 22:17, 19; 1 Cor 11:23–24; CCC 1359–1361.

acknowledge him, and he will make straight your paths. Be not wise in your own eyes; fear the LORD, and turn away from evil. (3:5–7)

Happy is the man who finds wisdom, and the man who gets understanding, for the gain from it is better than gain from silver and its profit better than gold. (3:13, 14)

A man needs wisdom to make decisions every day. But possessing Christian wisdom is especially important because your eternal salvation is at stake. If you are a father, it is even more important because you are the shepherd and steward of *all* the souls in your home.

Wisdom does not stand alone, but is made possible by possessing the proper information. This is why Paul prays that we will receive revelation. Paul is not talking about divine Revelation; rather, he means understanding. The word "revelation" in the original Greek means "to unveil," "to lay bare," or "to make known the truth." Paul knows that the truth must be laid bare and unveiled for us before we can act in wisdom. Only after we clearly see the truth can we grow in wisdom.

Paul is not asking God to give worldly wisdom and revelation, but wisdom and revelation in the knowledge of God. Since God is the author of all things sacred and secular, the key to having wisdom in secular affairs, such as business, finances, and recreation, is to be rooted in a proper understanding of God. If we make the proper investment into our Christian faith, we will reap rewards that impact every aspect of our life.

## Knowing Hope | Verse 18

**"HAVING THE EYES OF YOUR HEARTS ENLIGHTENED, THAT YOU MAY KNOW WHAT IS THE HOPE TO WHICH HE HAS CALLED YOU, WHAT ARE THE RICHES OF HIS GLORIOUS INHERITANCE IN THE SAINTS."**

The word "hope" gets a bad rap in modern English. There is a great difference between the modern understanding of hope and the biblical understanding of hope. The modern usage translates more like "wishful thinking." We say, "I hope I win the lottery." "I hope my team wins the Super Bowl." "I hope I lose weight on this pizza and beer diet." That kind of hope is rooted in chance, and we are truly surprised if our wish comes true.

Biblical hope is completely different. Paul is praying that, through the wisdom and revelation of God, our spiritual eyes will be opened so we will *know the hope to which we have been called*. What is this hope? Salvation in Christ. Paul says to the Thessalonians, "let us be sober, and put on the breastplate of faith and love, and for a helmet the hope of salvation" (1 Thess 5:8).

The proper understanding of biblical hope is "confident expectation." Hope does deal with things that we have yet to possess (see Rom 8:24–25), but our expectation of receiving that for which we hope is based on confidence in God and not on chance. In Romans Paul says, "Hope does not disappoint us, because God's love has been poured into our hearts through the Holy Spirit who has been given to us" (5:5).

Paul wants you to know that if you are in Christ, you can have confidence in your salvation. You do not need to hope, as in wishful thinking, that God will accept your faith, that Baptism will work, or that forgiveness truly comes in the Sacrament of Penance. Our hope in God is a confident expectation that what He says will come to pass. When you invest in Christ, there is no wondering "if" it will work, because our hope is rooted in God, who never changes (see Heb 13:8).

## Knowing Power | Verse 19

**"AND WHAT IS THE IMMEASURABLE GREATNESS OF HIS POWER IN US WHO BELIEVE, ACCORDING TO THE WORKING OF HIS GREAT MIGHT."**

Men love power. A lot is good and more is better, even when buying a lawn mower. You might be looking at a 5-hp mower that is perfect for your yard. Then you catch sight of a 6.5-hp mower and can't help but think that the extra 1.5-hp will really make a difference in your 400-square-foot yard.

Paul wants you to be confident in the hope of your salvation and to know the great power of God within you as a Christian. When you were baptized, you received the power of God in your soul. When you were confirmed, this initial deposit of God was completed. When you made your First Communion, God's power continued to strengthen you with the Eucharist. Jesus said that we receive power when we receive the Holy Spirit (Acts 1:8). Paul seems to go overboard to indicate the greatness of this power within us, but if you are like the average guy, you don't feel very powerful.

What is this power? First and foremost, it is the grace of God within us that brings us to salvation. Without Christ you are separated from God and are incapable of reaching Him on your own. The greatness of God's power restores saving grace to us, conquers sin, and makes us sons of God. This power allows us to live victorious lives in Christ. Paul says that he can do all things through the strength of Christ (Phil 4:13). Through the power of Christ we can overcome sin and live the life God intends for us.

Paul does give one qualifier. This power will be present in those who believe. The sins against hope are despair and presumption (CCC 2091). When we despair we cease to believe that God will do what He has promised, and His power is unable to work through us. Presumption is when we no longer believe we need God or we believe that God will overlook our sins.

Paul is giving us the big picture in this first chapter of Ephesians and calling us to grow in understanding our faith so that we will fully believe in Jesus and live powerful lives in Christ.

## Power Brokers

It is always amazing to see how one individual can transform a company or a sports team. In 1996, Steve Jobs came back to Apple Computer and managed to take the company from near death to wild prosperity. In 2007, *Fortune* Magazine named Jobs the most powerful person in business. In the 1960s, Vince Lombardi transformed the Green Bay Packers from one of the worst teams in the NFL to one of the best teams of all time, winning five conference championships in seven years. Lombardi is often cited as the best NFL coach of all time. These kinds of men are those who know how to lead with authority, overcome adversity, and inspire others to become their best.

## Power through Brokenness | Verses 20–23

"WHICH HE ACCOMPLISHED IN CHRIST WHEN HE RAISED HIM FROM THE DEAD AND MADE HIM SIT AT HIS RIGHT HAND IN THE HEAVENLY PLACES, FAR ABOVE ALL RULE AND AUTHORITY AND POWER AND DOMINION, AND ABOVE EVERY NAME THAT IS NAMED, NOT ONLY IN THIS AGE BUT ALSO IN THAT WHICH IS TO COME; AND HE HAS PUT ALL THINGS UNDER HIS FEET AND HAS MADE HIM THE HEAD OVER ALL THINGS FOR THE CHURCH, WHICH IS HIS BODY, THE FULLNESS OF HIM WHO FILLS ALL IN ALL."

Paul finishes this first chapter with a summary of the amazing power and authority of Jesus Christ—the most powerful, transformative leader of all time. Jesus does not transform us through creative genius, dazzling personality, or rigorous workouts. He transforms us through His very person.

The work of Christ is not seen in spreadsheets or stats, but is found in restoring each person to his God given destiny: perfect unity with God. How did Christ do this? Through the Cross. Most leaders try to overcome adversity through their perceived strengths; Jesus conquered sin and death through a complete sacrifice of Himself. Paul tells us the result of this perfect sacrifice of the sinless Son of God.

Jesus:
> Sits at the right hand of God the Father in heaven;
> Is far above all rule, authority, power and dominion;

> Is the name higher than any other name;
> Has authority on earth and in heaven;
> Has had all things subjected to His authority;
> Is the head of the Church, which is truly His body.

When you call on the name of Jesus, you are not calling on one name among many other good options. You are calling upon the supreme authority of which there is no equal. When you embrace the Church, you are not just embracing a human institution. You are embracing the very person of Christ. Christ has all authority and He works through His Church, which embodies the fullness of Christ.

## Conclusion: Individual Retirement Accounts (IRA)

Invest for the long term. When you take the time to know Jesus Christ and to understand the faith, you are making a long-term investment that will impact every aspect of your earthly life. At some point you will permanently retire (die). When that time comes, you will receive a full return on your investments made in this life. You don't want to find that you failed to make spiritual deposits while you had the chance.

Christ is the best investment you could ever make, because Christ is eternal. If you only invest in the temporary things of this world, you set yourself on very unstable ground (see Mt 7:24–29). To invest well, begin with thankfulness, and then pursue understanding the Christian faith and knowledge of the hope and power of Christ. Pursue this with firm belief that Jesus is the name above all names, to whom all things have been subjected, and that the Catholic Church is the place where the fullness of Christ is found.

## Study Questions

1. Have you ever lost your shirt because of a poorly researched decision? Explain.

2. Understanding your Christian faith is important for success and satisfaction in every area of life. In which area do you most need increased success and satisfaction: work, money, recreation, friends, family, marriage, or sexuality? Circle one.

3. How can you know if you are truly thankful for God's blessings?

4. Do you really believe you will have more success in your secular affairs when you have a better understanding of God? Why or why not?

5. Do you have confidence that you possess salvation? Why?

6. Have you ever found yourself in despair? What brought you out of it?

7. Whom do you admire most as an example of a powerful leader? Give an example from sports, business, or others.

8. How do you most often measure success in your life: money, promotion, approval?

9. Do you feel you are making good eternal deposits and investments? Explain.

# CHAPTER 3

# Great Comebacks

You were dead in sin, but made alive through Jesus
EPHESIANS 2:1–10

Everyone loves a winner—a true champion who brings power, elegance, and character to his game. Eventually, all great champions retire. But occasionally, after some time passes, a champion realizes there is more left in the tank and a comeback is born. One of the more dramatic comeback stories in recent history is the return of Michael Jordan to the NBA in 1995.

After leading the Chicago Bulls to three NBA championships, and himself winning seven consecutive scoring titles and three straight Finals MVP awards, Michael Jordan retired in October 1993. Personal issues in his life played heavily into this decision, not the least of which was the murder of his father the previous July.

Jordan, not content to sit on the sidelines, tried his hand at minor league baseball with less than stellar success. A year and a half after leaving the game of basketball, Jordan issues a two-word press release, "I'm back." He returns to the ailing Chicago Bulls in the middle of the 1994–95 season giving them hope for a better future.

Upon his return, the sports world buzzes with speculation as to whether the old Jordan still exists. Jordan, now thirty-two, is not as spry as he was in his twenties. His first few games are good, but not great. Jordan is finding his place on the new team and adjusting his game to match his age. In his fourth game back,

Jordan hits a winning shot at the buzzer, giving everyone a glimpse of things to come.

In his fifth game back, the Bulls play the New York Knicks at Madison Square Garden. The Knicks are the number one defensive team that season. Only one player has scored more than forty points against them (Shaq, forty-one) and only three others scored more than thirty. It would be against this team, on this grand stage, that Jordan makes clear to the world that he is in fact "back."

Jordan steps onto the court and wastes no time, hitting his first jumper, then another, and another. Bulls and Knicks fans alike watch in wonder as Jordan takes command of the court. By the end of the first period, he has twenty points. As the game progresses, Jordan hits short and long-range jumpers, three point shots, and the occasional dunk. He forces turnovers, grabs rebounds, and commits only two turnovers.

By the fourth quarter, anticipation of a fifty-point game is building. No one has ever scored more than fifty points against the Knicks in the Garden. One shot after another continues to fall. With 25.8 seconds left, Jordan sets a new Garden scoring record of fifty-five points.

But more drama is yet to come.

With 14.6 seconds left in the game, the Bulls and Knicks are tied at 111. The Bulls have possession and inbound the ball to Jordan. Hot all night, Jordan is frequently double-teamed. A minute earlier, Patrick Ewing had left his man and blocked one of Jordan's shots. This block is firmly in the mind of Jordan.

He moves up the court toward his defender. He fakes right, then left, and drives hard into the paint. Jordan spins, goes up for the shot, and sees Ewing coming in for the block. This means one thing: Ewing's man is open. Jordan elevates for the shot and passes the ball to the open man under the basket, who dunks the ball and wins the game.

Jordan is back! Older, wiser, smarter, and ready to win—again. The ailing Bulls are resurrected and Jordan's comeback is legit. The next season the Bulls would set the record for the best single season ever in the NBA and would go on to win another three straight championships.

## Death Defying

Why do we like comeback stories? Because they give us hope. In some sense, we like to imagine ourselves in the story and relish the thought of being that guy—the one who overcomes the odds to accomplish the impossible.

At the close of chapter one in Ephesians, Paul directs our attention to the greatest comeback story of all time: the Resurrection of Jesus Christ. Imagine for a moment what it would have been like to watch Jesus die. He does not die a "normal" death. He was brutally scourged, beaten, and then nailed to a cross through His hands and feet. Hanging on the Cross, the weight of His body makes it difficult to breath and a combination of dehydration, blood loss, and asphyxiation brings about a slow and painful death. Finally, He is pierced by a spear and blood and water flow from His side to confirm His death.

If you were one of His followers at that time, there is no way you would have expected Jesus to be alive and in good health just three days later. It would be absolutely impossible, that is, impossible through the natural power of man, but very possible through the supernatural power of God (Mt 19:26). Reflecting on the crucifixion and Resurrection of Christ is key to understanding why the Apostles, like Paul, vigorously preached the Gospel. They watched Jesus perform many miracles, but nothing compared to exiting the grave after three days. Jesus had overcome many obstacles while He was with them, but this was something completely different.

They saw Jesus conquer death!

Everyone knows you can't cheat death, but Jesus didn't cheat it. He beat it. This victory caused the Apostle John to write in the opening verses of his first letter:

That . . . which we have heard, which we have

seen with our eyes, which we have looked upon and touched with our hands, concerning the word of life—the life was made manifest, and we saw it, and testify to it, and proclaim to you the eternal life which was with the Father and was made manifest to us—that which we have seen and heard we proclaim also to you, so that you may have fellowship with us; and our fellowship is with the Father and with his Son Jesus Christ. (1 Jn 1:1–3)

When ordered to stop preaching about Jesus by the governing authorities, Peter and John will proclaim together, "We cannot stop speaking about what we have seen and heard" (Acts 4:20). The bodily Resurrection of Christ is the greatest comeback story of all time and it is the reason that we have the Christian faith today.

## Dead on Arrival (DOA)

In the beginning, Adam and Eve were created sinless and full of God's grace. God told Adam that the penalty for sin would be death (Gen 2:17). Adam sinned and immediately experienced spiritual death, and physical death entered into the world for the first time (note the spiritual came before the physical). Adam's spiritual death came through the loss of God's saving grace in his soul, which meant everyone born after Adam would not possess God's saving grace in their soul, but instead inherit a fallen human nature inclined toward sin. The Church calls this lack of saving grace at birth "original sin." Original sin is not a sin committed, as in a personal fault, but the lack of God's saving grace in us at birth (CCC 405–406).

The result is that every person is born separated from God. In essence, we are DOA. We are not guilty of personal sin until we commit an actual sin, but sooner or later everyone commits a personal sin. We are born enslaved to spiritual and physical death. It bears repeating that this is a supernatural spiritual condition that can be fixed only by something outside of the natural order. Only the One who created life and conquered death can restore what was lost. Left to ourselves, we would live lives full of sin and die separated from God forever.

### But Wait, There's More! | Verses 1–2 and 5–6

"AND YOU HE MADE ALIVE, WHEN YOU WERE DEAD THROUGH THE TRESPASSES AND SINS IN WHICH YOU ONCE WALKED, FOLLOWING THE COURSE OF THIS WORD, FOLLOWING THE PRINCE OF THE POWER OF THE AIR, THE SPIRIT THAT IS NOW AT WORK IN THE SONS OF DISOBEDIENCE . . . EVEN WHEN WE WERE DEAD THROUGH OUR TRESPASSES, MADE US ALIVE TOGETHER WITH CHRIST (BY GRACE YOU HAVE BEEN SAVED), AND RAISED US UP WITH HIM, AND MADE US SIT WITH HIM IN THE HEAVENLY PLACES IN CHRIST JESUS."

To us, overcoming our spiritual condition can seem as impossible as Jesus rising from the dead. Death appears too strong. With all of this in mind, Paul speaks words of encouragement as he reminds us of the profound work of Jesus Christ: While you were dead in sin, you were made alive with Christ. If you are a Christian, you are living a comeback story and sharing in the greatest comeback story of all time, the Resurrection of Jesus Christ.

Jesus conquered death for all people, not just for Himself. The miracle is that Jesus' Resurrection from the dead has made possible your resurrection from the dead. Just like Adam, you receive the spiritual before the physical. When you become a Christian, you become immediately spiritually alive, because spiritual death is conquered. Paul says that you have been raised with Christ and sit in the heavenly places. You are sharing in the sonship of Jesus. After you physically die, when Christ restores all things, you will physically rise from the dead and be united, body and soul, in heaven for all eternity. Physical death is conquered (CCC 1004, 1042).

## Amazing Grace | Verses 4–9

What must we do to receive this? How do we receive this gift of life? What does it mean for us?

First, the gift of life we receive through Jesus is called grace, or more specifically, sanctifying grace. Sanctifying grace is the grace that saves us, the very divine life of God living in us (CCC Glossary: Grace). Why does God do this? Because He is "rich in mercy" and has "great love" for us. Since you are a son, God knows you (Jer 1:5 and Ps 139:13) and desires that you should come to know Him personally.

What must we do to receive this grace? Nothing. Paul makes it very clear that there is nothing you can do to earn this initial gift of grace. It is a gratuitous gift of God to you (CCC 1999, 2010). Remember, before you receive this gift you are dead, and a dead man cannot act. The only thing a dead man can "do" is passively receive. If receiving this grace was based on how good you could be, then you could boast or take credit for possessing this great gift, like the football player who showboats after making a touchdown. What makes grace so amazing is that God gives it to us while we are dead in our sin and completely undeserving.

How do we receive this grace? We receive it through faith and Baptism.[1] If you were baptized as an infant, you received the power of the living God within your soul the moment you were baptized. As a baby, you had no personal sin to impede your reception of grace. If you were baptized as an adult, repentance had to precede faith and Baptism, because you can only be forgiven if you are truly sorry for your sin.

What does this mean for us? Grace places God's divine life within us, and therefore He provides us the power needed to live this life, the power to make our comeback and winning season! God desires you to thrive in this life, not simply survive. This does not mean that God's grace controls you like a robot. You must cooperate with God's grace for it to bring the greatest results. God is the coach and you are the player. You will only win the game if you run the plays He calls.

---

1. Mk 16:16; Acts 2:38; Gal 3:26–27; 1 Pet 3:21; CCC 1253, 1257.

## Going the Distance | Verses 2–3 and 10

"[YOU WERE DEAD THROUGH THE TRESPASSES AND SINS] IN WHICH YOU ONCE WALKED, FOLLOWING THE COURSE OF THIS WORLD, FOLLOWING THE PRINCE OF THE POWER OF THE AIR, THE SPIRIT THAT IS NOW AT WORK IN THE SONS OF DISOBEDIENCE. AMONG THESE WE ALL ONCE LIVED IN THE PASSIONS OF OUR FLESH, FOLLOWING THE DESIRES OF BODY AND MIND, AND SO WE WERE BY NATURE CHILDREN OF WRATH, LIKE THE REST OF MANKIND. . . . FOR WE ARE HIS WORKMANSHIP, CREATED IN CHRIST JESUS FOR GOOD WORKS, WHICH GOD PREPARED BEFOREHAND, THAT WE SHOULD WALK IN THEM."

There are many great stories about how a new coach takes over an undisciplined, losing team and turns them into winners. There is usually a consistent theme in these stories. The coach comes in and takes the team back to basics. He drills the fundamentals into them. He gets their conditioning up and teaches them to follow his playbook. Those who buck the system get extra conditioning or, in extreme cases, are dismissed from the team. The players dislike the coach in the beginning because he makes them work hard and follow the rules. But once the team starts winning, the players come to respect the coach, see the wisdom of his methods, and are able to go the distance.

While God's grace is a gratuitous, free gift, Paul teaches us that this grace should bring about an active response. We can never earn the initial grace of salvation, but once we are in Christ, Paul says we should do good works and that God created us for this very purpose. To be a Christian and not do good works is like being a football running back who never runs plays.

Paul will outline some of these good works later in Ephesians, but suffice it to say that good works are like God's playbook. The good works He calls us to are, in fact, work: They don't usually come easy and often require sacrifice. But, like the team that listens to the new coach even though it's hard, we will be on a winning team if we follow God's instructions.

Throughout the New Testament, those who follow Christ are identified by their faith or belief. Those who reject God are identified by their disobedience (Heb 11:31; Tit 1:16; Jn 3:16). Paul highlights both of these actions in this section. Those who reject God and follow their own plans are called the "sons of disobedience"—they refuse to listen to the coach. Those who are saved by grace have come through faith. True faith always includes action. It is completely foreign to Scripture and historic Christian teaching to separate faith from works. Faith must come first, but it is completed by good works (Jas 2:22–24).

## Conclusion

Great comebacks are always exciting to watch and even more exciting to live. Jesus defeated the ultimate foe—death—and staged a comeback that will only be exceeded by His return at the end of time. As a Christian, you share in Christ's Resurrection because God, by His grace, has placed His divine life in you, conquering sin and death in you. God has given you this profound gift so you can live a victorious life, free from the disobedience caused by sin.

Whether you feel victorious or not, stand up and accept the reality of your situation. You have been brought from death to life and are a son of God. If your life is not marked by good works consistent with Christian living, make a thorough examination of conscience, get to Confession, and ask for God's forgiveness. He will never turn you away. He may have you run some extra laps (penance) for your disobedience (Heb 12:5–11), but never forget that God is "rich in mercy" and does everything out of "great love" for you.

## Study Questions

1. Name and comment on two aspects of spiritual death:

a.



b.




2. Name three good works that have not been in your life to date that you could add to your playbook:

a.



b.



c.

3. What were you like before your "comeback" story?

CHAPTER 4

# Strength through Peace

The power of the Cross brings peace between men and peace
between mankind and God
EPHESIANS 2:11–22

The day was like any other winter day in the San Joaquin valley, mid-40s, overcast, and heading toward rain. Jake had a simple assignment: Take Ryan to the orthodontist during the last period of the day. The two young men were seniors in high school and excited to be excused from school to take care of this "special mission." This really wasn't a mission, nor was it special, but most high school boys are prone to add "special mission" to just about any project so it will have a more "covert" feel.

Jake was something of a gear-head and really liked off-road vehicles. Unfortunately, his car was a standard 1966 Bug with chrome wheels and sparkling, metallic rust paint. Even though his Bug wasn't truly dirt worthy, Jake could often be found doing donuts in nearby fields. This is where the story takes a detour.

The boys leave campus and drive through the outskirts of town toward the orthodontist. As they drive, Jake reminds Ryan that they will soon pass a field that has a huge pit with 45-degree sides. By this time it has begun to rain and they realize that their "special mission" would be much improved with a brief detour.

They enter the field and the mud flinging begins. Jake drives down into the pit, splashes through the puddle and up the other side, airing out the front tires. The adrenaline begins to flow. After multiple runs, Jake's confidence in his Bug's capabilities begins to grow. Jake heads into the open field, doing doughnuts and flinging mud everywhere, when something starts to go wrong. His Bug begins to remind him that it is, in fact, not mud worthy.

The car goes slower, and slower, and slower as it sinks into the mud. Finally the wheels are spinning, but the Bug is not moving. They are stuck.

Since it is Jake's car, Ryan has to get out in the mud and push. He pushes with all his might, but to no avail. They look at each other and suddenly realize that they are AWOL from their "special mission" to the orthodontist.

Desperate for options, Jake looks across the field and sees a construction site with a Ford F150 4x4. The boys walk to the site and ask the owner of the truck if he would pull Jake's Bug out of the mud. Of course, like any self-respecting man, the 4x4 guy sees "special mission" flash through his mind and agrees to rescue the Bug. Whatever thwarted the wimpy Bug will be no match for his mighty Ford.

The Ford bravely heads into the field while the boys eagerly look on, smiling. They watch the mighty Ford gracefully glide across the field and easily pass the location of the Bug when it suddenly begins to go slower, and slower, and slower, and sinks to its axles. The next two hours are spent in the pouring rain shoveling, wedging, pushing, and jacking, but the truck only sinks deeper into the mud.

Reinforcement is requested by cell phone. A huge tow truck arrives and hooks a cable to the Ford. The winch starts, but the wrong truck moves! The Ford is so seriously stuck that the tow truck is being pulled into the mud instead of the Ford being pulled out. Jake and Ryan begin to worry. The tow truck operator places chocks in front of his wheels, tries again, but yields the same results. The Ford is really, really, stuck.

Finally, the operator sees a large dirt mound and gets an idea. He drives his truck behind the dirt mound to use it as a stop. He runs out the cables, turns on the winch, and finally the Ford begins to move. It torques and twists as it is pulled from its muddy resting place. Victory!

In the end, the Ford needed a power much greater than its own to be set free. Without the tow truck, all the efforts of Jake and Ryan simply made the situation worse. There was no way they could help themselves. They were helpless on their own.

### Going Nowhere Fast

Why don't men like to ask for directions when they are lost? In general, because men don't like to appear weak. We often believe that weakness is okay for the other gender, but not for men. If something breaks, we can fix it. If something is stuck, we'll get it loose. If we're lost, one more trip around the block will make things clear. Asking for help is often the last resort because it is an admission of weakness that I cannot do this on my own. Admitting need of any kind requires humility and keeping pride in check. This is not an easy thing to do, especially for men.

In this section, Paul builds upon his teaching that without Christ we are dead in our sin, and adds that we have no hope (Eph 2:12). Paul's goal is not to depress us, but to help us see that we truly *need* Jesus. Without Jesus, we are like the driver who was asked where he was going and replied, "I don't know, but I'm making good time!" Thankfully, Paul does not leave us in this place of despair, but goes on to tell us how and why this is not the case for the Christian. Once again, he roots us in the big picture and helps us see that Christ is the key to everything.

### Oil and Water | Verses 11–12

"THEREFORE REMEMBER THAT AT ONE TIME YOU GENTILES IN THE FLESH, CALLED THE UNCIRCUMCISION BY WHAT IS CALLED THE CIRCUMCISION, WHICH IS MADE IN THE FLESH BY HANDS—REMEMBER THAT YOU WERE AT THAT TIME SEPARATED FROM CHRIST, ALIENATED FROM THE COMMONWEALTH OF ISRAEL, AND STRANGERS TO THE

**COVENANTS OF PROMISE, HAVING NO HOPE AND WITHOUT GOD IN THE WORLD."**

Paul introduces us to tension between Jews (circumcision) and Gentiles (uncircumcision, non-Jews) and between man and God. What happens when you mix oil and water? The oil stays together and will not blend with the water. This is like the relationship between the Jews and Gentiles. They lived in the same city, but had little interaction. In fact, Jews believed that they had been forbidden by God to associate with Gentiles (see Acts 10:28; Deut 7:2–3).

First, Paul reminds us of the privileged place of Israel as the chosen people. God chose Israel to be His people, and they were the first to hear the Word of God (CCC 62–64). You could say that Israel received a prescreening of God's plan of salvation. Once Jesus came, many in Israel believed because they had been anticipating the coming of the Messiah (Jesus).

Second, in the strongest language possible, Paul makes it clear that the Gentiles are the complete opposite of the Jews. The Gentiles did not have the benefit of God's direct Revelation and were completely separated from God. He drives home the point by saying they were without "hope and without God in the world." To what hope is Paul referring? The hope of salvation. On their own, Gentiles did not have access to God's plan of salvation.

Even though Jews had the advantage of God's Revelation, they were no more capable of saving themselves than the Gentiles. Just like the Ford stuck in the mud, no man has any hope of rescuing himself from his sin. Every man must recognize he needs something he cannot provide.

## There's Power in the Blood | Verse 13

**"BUT NOW IN CHRIST JESUS YOU WHO ONCE WERE FAR OFF HAVE BEEN BROUGHT NEAR IN THE BLOOD OF CHRIST."**

In verses eleven and twelve, Paul focuses on those who are not in Christ. In verse thirteen, he moves to those for whom the situation is much different, those who have believed in Jesus and been baptized. The blood of Christ, shed on the Cross, is what each man needs and cannot provide himself. Because of our sin we were separated from God by a chasm we cannot traverse. Through Adam's sin we lost God's saving grace, and only God could restore His grace. And, thanks be to God, through the blood of Christ, we who were once separated from God have been brought near to God through the Cross. Where there was once separation, there is now unity through Christ Jesus. Instead of hopelessness, we are filled with a "confident expectation" of our coming salvation.

God told Adam that the penalty for sin would be death, and God sent His own Son to pay that penalty (CCC Glossary: "Redeemer/Redemption"). This means that God, through Jesus Christ, has made it possible for you to know Him, and therefore to find the true purpose for your life. Every time you go to Mass, Jesus' sacrifice on the Cross is re-presented before your eyes in the Eucharist, reminding you how much God loves you and wants to know you. Every time you receive the Body and Blood of Jesus at Mass, God is once again bringing you near so you can live as He intended, in deep union with Jesus as a son of God and full heir to His kingdom (CCC 460, 1391).

## The Power of Peace | Verses 14–18

When it comes to movies, men usually choose action over romance. Many men have unsuccessfully held their tongue as they dutifully sat with their wife through a chick flick. At some point in the movie, the husband can't take it anymore and is driven to blurt out, "Why doesn't she just say what she thinks. If it were two men, they'd say what they think, exchange a few blows, and then go for a beer. Man, I'm glad I'm not a woman!" Men would much rather watch a guy take charge, track down the villain, and dispense justice with a few explosions along the way. We like action because we like to see things get done and we respect strong leadership.

Because of our desire for action, we can sometimes miss the power of Jesus' work on the Cross. A story where the good guy conquers by allowing the enemy to kill him is not the standard story line. The Resurrection is a powerful scene, but if Hollywood had made the story, Jesus would have busted out of the grave, flown through Jerusalem, and put the smackdown on everyone who sent Him to the Cross.

What is it Jesus came to do? He came to conquer sin and death. Jesus did not come to conquer people, but to save them. The story of Jesus is the greatest action adventure ever told, but God's methods are not the same as ours. God delights in bringing victory in ways that seem backward to human logic so that the victory will truly be credited to Him (1 Cor 1:20–31). When talking about how foolish the story of the Cross seems to the world, Paul tells the Church in Corinth that "God chose what is foolish in the world to shame the wise, God chose what is weak in the world to shame the strong . . . so that no human being might boast in the presence of God . . . therefore, as it is written, 'Let him who boasts, boast of the Lord'" (1 Cor 1:27, 29, 31).

With this in mind, Paul gives us this profound statement: Jesus is our peace.

Paul does not say that Jesus shows us the way to peace, but that Jesus *is* peace. The person of Christ brought peace to humanity. The actions of Christ brought peace to humanity. Jesus didn't come to wage a physical war with physical weapons, but a spiritual war with spiritual weapons. He endured the worst physical abuse humanity could deliver so that He could conquer the violence of sin through the power of peace. Instead of revenge, Jesus chose forgiveness. This is powerfully seen when Jesus, while hanging on the Cross, asks God the Father to forgive those who are crucifying Him (Lk 22:34).

What does this peace bring? Paul highlights two specific results of the peace that comes through Jesus.

### Peace Between All Men

First, Paul tells us that through Christ, the barrier that once existed between Jews and the rest of humanity has been destroyed.

There was a time when only the Jews had the commandments of God and the laws prescribing proper worship of Him. But Jesus abolished the old law, allowing Jews and Gentiles to have equal access to God and to be one through Christ. The law previously given was to prepare for the coming of the Christ (Jesus). Once He came, the old law was no longer needed because Christ fulfilled all of the requirements of the law in His life, death, and Resurrection. Those who are saved by the blood of Jesus are now called Christians, whether they were previously a Jew or a Gentile. To be a Christian is not a nationality, but a spiritual reality. It is a person who is in Christ. The peace that comes through Jesus is able to transcend any nation, race, or gender. Paul says, "There is neither Jew nor Greek, there is neither slave nor free, there is neither male nor female; for you are all one in Christ Jesus" (Gal 3:28).

## Peace Between Mankind and God

As a result of the Fall, all men—Jews and Gentiles—needed to be reconciled to God. The ravages of sin had caused hostility to exist between man and God, but when Christ conquered sin, He made it possible for man to commune with God once again. Paul says that Jesus preached peace to those who were far off (Gentiles) and to those who were near (Jews), and reconciled them both to God so that hostility would cease between men and between mankind and God.

The key to living a blessed life is to know God, and the peace of Christ makes this possible. Paul tells us that through Jesus we now have access to God the Father in the Spirit. Since there is no longer hostility between a Christian man and God, we are now free to learn from God how to be what He created us to be, whether we're married or single, a priest or teacher, a businessman or inventor, a father, husband, etc.

### Peace Be with You

Jesus accomplished more through peace than physical aggression could ever accomplish. This should transform how we "pass the peace" at Mass. Notice how often peace is mentioned during Mass. It is everywhere. Most notably, right before we give each other the sign of peace, the priest says,

> Lord Jesus Christ,
> who said to your Apostles:
> Peace I leave you, my peace I give you;[1]
> look not on our sins, but on
> the faith of your Church,
> and graciously grant her peace and unity
> in accordance with your will.
> Who live and reign for ever and ever.

The peace of Christ has made life worth living. Next time you are at Mass and turn to give the sign of peace, look the person in the eye for an extra second and say with conviction, "Peace be with you." If you want to go for maximum impact you can say, "May the peace of Christ be with you," and don't let go of their hand until you're finished. They'll probably give you a strange look, but that's okay. It will make them think.

### Coming Home | Verses 19–22

"SO THEN YOU ARE NO LONGER STRANGERS AND SOJOURNERS, BUT YOU ARE FELLOW CITIZENS WITH THE SAINTS AND MEMBERS OF THE HOUSEHOLD OF GOD, BUILT UPON THE FOUNDATION OF THE APOSTLES AND PROPHETS, CHRIST JESUS HIMSELF BEING THE CORNERSTONE, IN WHOM THE WHOLE STRUCTURE IS JOINED TOGETHER AND GROWS INTO A HOLY TEMPLE IN THE LORD; IN WHOM YOU ALSO ARE BUILT INTO IT FOR A DWELLING PLACE OF GOD IN THE SPIRIT."

---

1. Jn 14:27; cf. Jn 16:33; 20:19–26.

Finally, at the end of this section, Paul brings us back to our place in the big picture. Through Christ we are now a part of God's family, no longer outsiders but full members of God's household, with full access to all that God possesses. Keeping the Jews in mind, Paul reminds us that this plan is not new but is what the prophets proclaimed for centuries before Christ. The Apostles revealed the full extent of God's saving work, which, as always, places Christ as the cornerstone of God's plan of salvation. As it is impossible to remove the foundation of a building without destroying the building, if you remove Christ, the entire structure crumbles. Christ is the Rock that allows everyone to stand on unshakable ground.

## Conclusion

Part of growing into full manhood is learning how to make tough decisions. One of the toughest decisions you can make is to acknowledge that you need Jesus. You might have been baptized as a baby and, while you truly received the grace of Christ at that time, you might never have personally acknowledged your need for Him.

Once you can acknowledge your helplessness and accept Christ as your answer, you can fully participate in the power of the blood of Christ. This process can feel counterintuitive to our natural desire to fix things on our own, but when you submit to Christ, you find an unshakeable strength coming through the peace of Christ. You can fully become what God created you to be. Do not forget, you are a son, an heir to God's household with full access to all that God possesses.

## Study Questions

1. Give an example from your own life where you were seriously aware of needing a power greater than your own. What happened?

2. Have you come to the conclusion yet that you need something in your life you cannot provide? Explain.

3. When you partake of the Eucharist, do you feel or experience a movement toward God? Why or why not?

4. Has the peace of God in your life helped you to forgive some significant person? Who is that person?

5. In what ways does knowing God remove hostility or anger in your life?

CHAPTER 5

# Search and Rescue

Through the Church, God proclaimed the mystery of the
Gospel to the world
EPHESIANS 3

Deep in the mountainous jungles of Colombia, prisoners are
roused for an early morning march. They will be relocating to a new
camp today. They are not moved by boat or truck, but through an
arduous all-day march with their hands and feet bound. Humidity
is high, mosquitoes are thick, and the heat makes the already weak
prisoners weaker still.

The prisoners are hostages captured by the Revolutionary Armed
Forces of Colombia (FARC, from the Spanish *Fuerzas Armadas
Revolucionarias de Colombia*) to help them advance their radical
political agenda. Within the group are three American military
contractors, eleven Colombian military and police, and a woman
politician who previously ran for president in Colombia. Most of the
hostages have been held captive for more than five years. They have
been subjected to isolation, deplorable conditions, and constant
mind games used by FARC leaders trying to maintain control.

Eventually, Colombian and American officials cooperate on
a daring search-and-rescue mission. The terrain of the jungle
makes finding FARC hideouts extremely difficult, and the constant
movement of the hostages means one thing: The only way to get
accurate intelligence is from within FARC. The whole endeavor is

complicated because FARC is a well-armed operation.

Through U.S. spy satellites and other surveillance technology, the Colombian government tracks the location of FARC cells. The next step is to infiltrate. A full year before launching a rescue effort, the Colombian government inserts a mole into the FARC forces. The first challenge is to locate the hostages. After eight months the hostages are located, but there is a problem: They are in different camps. The mole gains the trust of high-ranking officials and eventually convinces them to group the hostages into one location.

Colombian officials see FARC's frequent movement of the hostages as an opportunity. Operatives are to pose as a friendly international nongovernmental organization (NGO) that will transport the hostages from one camp to another. To build credibility, the mole convinces the FARC guerillas to move the hostages to the camp of the FARC leader, Alfonso Cano.

Colombian officials, posing as the fake NGO, make contact with FARC and offer to fly the hostages to the new location. The FARC leaders agree. To prepare for the meeting the soldiers take acting classes to convincingly play their parts during the transfer. Two soldiers pose as a cameraman and journalist, two as fellow FARC guerillas, and others as aid workers.

On July 2, 2008, the rescue plan is launched. The hostages hope they might be participating in a prisoner exchange, but when they arrive to see unmarked helicopters and FARC military on board, their hearts sink. The hostages are brought into the clearing and the Colombian operatives exit the helicopter to make contact. The mole, who is with the hostages, gives confirmation signals that only the rescuers can understand.

The hostages are loaded onto the helicopter and two real FARC guerillas are persuaded to board as well. Once in the air, things move so fast that the hostages have no idea what is happening. The FARC guerillas are persuaded to set aside their weapons. Suddenly they find themselves on the floor bound and blindfolded. Then the announcement comes, "We are the national army. You are free!" The hostages are stunned. After years in captivity, the entire rescue effort succeeds without firing a single shot.

## Global Search and Rescue

It is amazing to read search-and-rescue stories and realize how many people can be involved in saving a few lives. For the FARC hostage rescue, the governments of two countries worked together so that fifteen people could be liberated. Almost as many rescuers risked their lives to save the hostages (not to mention the mole who lived with FARC for more than a year). A successful rescue brings emotions of joy, thankfulness, appreciation, and humility, upon realizing that so much effort went into saving one life.

Paul closes the first half of Ephesians by bringing to light the grand search-and-rescue plan of God. This plan is not just for a small group of people and not simply for all humanity in a general, collective way, but for each individual person there ever was and ever will be, including you and me, in particular and by name. In the first three chapters of Ephesians, Paul is trying to deepen our spiritual understanding so we will have what we need to live the Christian life, which he will unfold in the last three chapters. An important aspect of our spiritual formation is an understanding of our place in God's grand scheme. We have said repeatedly that without Christ we are lost and without hope, but through Christ we are reunited to God. In this third chapter, Paul reveals more clearly God's global search-and-rescue plan to help all people come to know God's love and that the key to everything is Christ.

## Mystery: Clarity or Confusion? | Verses 3–5

**"THE MYSTERY WAS MADE KNOWN TO ME BY REVELATION, AS I HAVE WRITTEN BRIEFLY. WHEN YOU READ THIS YOU CAN PERCEIVE MY INSIGHT INTO THE MYSTERY OF CHRIST, WHICH WAS NOT MADE KNOWN TO THE SONS OF MEN OF OTHER GENERATIONS AS IT HAS NOW BEEN REVEALED TO HIS HOLY APOSTLES AND PROPHETS BY THE SPIRIT."**

What comes to mind when you hear the word "mystery"? We usually equate mystery with confusion or something unclear. A murder mystery novel is a mystery precisely because the answer to the problem is unknown and the adventure is in finding the answer. We rarely equate mystery with clarity.

Recall that at the beginning of Ephesians Paul introduces us to the "mystery of God's will" (Eph 1:9). Paul references mystery three times in this third chapter and he will come back to mystery two more times. The word "mystery" is used frequently in our Catholic faith. At the very beginning of Mass in the Penitential Rite, the priest says, "Let us acknowledge our sins, and so prepare ourselves to celebrate the sacred mysteries." And during the liturgy of the Eucharist, just after the consecration of the bread and wine, the priest invites the people to proclaim, "The mystery of faith."

If mystery equals something we don't know, then we are in trouble, because at Mass we're preparing to celebrate the mystery of Christ. After the priest invites the faithful to proclaim the mystery of faith, the faithful respond by declaring the content of the mystery, "We proclaim your death, O Lord, and profess your Resurrection until you come again."

At Mass we worship what is known, not what is unknown.

Here is a definition of mystery in its Christian context: Something we could not have known unless God revealed it; something we can understand but not fully (CCC 237). For Paul, the central theme of mystery is something we *can* know, not what is unknown. True, at one time the mystery was unknown, but now God has revealed it to Paul and the other Apostles. We could only know this mystery through God's Revelation. No amount of reasoned reflection on the natural world around us could reveal God's plan of salvation. Without God explicitly revealing Himself to us, the mystery would have remained hidden.

## Mystery Revealed | Verse 6

**"THAT IS, HOW THE GENTILES ARE FELLOW HEIRS, MEMBERS OF THE SAME BODY, AND PARTAKERS OF THE PROMISE IN CHRIST JESUS THROUGH THE GOSPEL."**

If you haven't yet made the connection, when Paul mentions Gentiles he's likely talking about your heritage (a Gentile is anyone who is not a Jew). Unless you are Jewish by ancestry, your heritage is that of the Gentiles—separated from Christ and without hope. If you believe in Jesus and are baptized, you are no longer a Gentile, but a Christian.

What is the mystery now revealed to Paul? The mystery is that the Gentiles are fellow heirs of God's house, members of the Body of Christ, and have full access to the promises of Christ. No longer is the rest of the world (non-Jews) cut off from God. To understand the full weight of Paul's statement requires a sufficient cultural understanding of the Jewish mind.

For Paul to say that the Gentiles are equal heirs with the Jews would be like someone declaring that the entire world was now a part of your family, with full access to all the rights, privileges, and benefits of being a member of your family. In other words, you'd better rent a stadium for Christmas dinner. This would have been very difficult news for Jews of the first century to understand. They had existed for fifteen hundred years as God's chosen people, and now everyone is chosen! While this was always God's plan, it was new and startling information for the Jews.

### The Mission of the Mystery | Verses 7–9

"OF THIS GOSPEL I WAS MADE A MINISTER ACCORDING TO THE GIFT OF GOD'S GRACE WHICH WAS GIVEN ME BY THE WORKING OF HIS POWER. TO ME, THOUGH I AM THE VERY LEAST OF ALL THE SAINTS, THIS GRACE WAS GIVEN, TO PREACH TO THE GENTILES THE UNSEARCHABLE RICHES OF CHRIST, AND TO MAKE ALL MEN SEE WHAT IS THE PLAN OF THE MYSTERY HIDDEN FOR AGES IN GOD WHO CREATED ALL THINGS."

Paul now reveals that you are the subject of the search-and-rescue plan. You were held hostage by sin, and Paul was the mole dropped behind enemy lines to bring you the good news of salvation. His mission was to take the Gospel's message to the Gentiles so they would know the saving power of Jesus Christ.

The living God of the universe has been orchestrating all of human history so that *you* could personally know Him. Once Christ proclaimed the Gospel, God sent out search-and-rescue teams to find you and tell you the good news, that through Christ you can be forgiven and become an adopted son of God. It doesn't matter what part of the world you live in, God has left no stone unturned.

The scope of God's efforts to reveal Himself to you should cause you to be in awe of His lavish love for you. The thousands of men (bishops, priests, laymen) God has commissioned to reach out to you should be humbling. And just like any search-and-rescue mission, there are sacrifices and suffering. Paul says in verse one that he became a prisoner for Christ on behalf of the Gentiles, and in verse twelve he says that his suffering is for your glory.

This sacrifice continues to this day. Your priest has chosen not to get married so that he could serve Christ and His Church full time. Your bishop, also unmarried, faithfully tends the flock of the diocese and sees to it that you have a priest. There are lay people who freely give their time to teach children at Church or help adults grow in their faith. All of these people chose to serve others rather than serve themselves. May we never take this blessing for granted.

## Through the Church | Verses 10–12

Have you ever stopped to think about why we have a Church? Why is there a building? Why do we have bishops and priests? Have you ever thought about what the Church is? Our non-Catholic brothers and sisters in Christ generally view the Church as an invisible reality made up of anyone who professes faith in Jesus Christ. The Catholic view is much different.

To Catholics, the Church is a visible reality, established by Christ for a specific purpose. This understanding of the Church comes from Jesus: "You are Peter, and on this rock I will build my church, and the powers of death shall not prevail against it" (Mt 16:18). The Church has a visible head, Peter, and it will endure. Jesus also said that the Church has authority to decide disputes between believers, be they doctrinal or otherwise (Mt 18:15–18). Furthermore, for arbitration on matters between believers, the Church must be a visible place that people can find. Jesus first instructs the faithful to try and resolve the issue themselves, even with witnesses, but if they can't, then they should take the issue to the Church. The Church is more than simply a gathering of believers.

All of this lays the foundation for Paul's amazing statement about the Church. Why do we have the Church, and why is it visible? Because, says Paul, it is through the Church that the mystery of Christ is revealed. Without the Church the wisdom of God would not be known. Jesus did not simply proclaim the Gospel and hope that everyone would figure it out on their own. Instead, Jesus established the Church to safeguard and to powerfully preach the Gospel of Christ. According to Paul, the Church is the "pillar and bulwark of the truth" (1 Tim 3:15).

Paul finishes by saying that this is an eternal plan made possible through Jesus Christ, and that through Jesus Christ we have access to the Gospel. This access is not passive, but we can come boldly and confidently before God. Why? Because we are sons and full heirs.

## Strengthening the Inner Man | Verses 14–21

The older we get, the more creaks and cracks we hear as we walk around. As time wears on, we become very aware that our bodies will not last forever and that one day, physical death will take us from this earth. While there is a limit to the strength of our outer man, there is no limit to the strength of our inner man.

Paul finishes chapter three with a prayer asking the Father to strengthen our inner man with might through the Holy Spirit. These first three chapters of Ephesians are designed to help us understand who we are in Christ and what He has done for us. Thoroughly understanding the foundations of our faith is key for strengthening our inner man so we can live for Christ with our outer man. Like any good training program for athletes, we have been focusing on the fundamentals so we will be ready to go deeper when the time comes.

Paul finishes with a list of requests that he prays will come to fruition as the Holy Spirit strengthens our inner man. Paul prays that:

> Christ may dwell in your heart through faith;
> You would be grounded in love;
> You would comprehend the fullness of Christ;
> You would know the love of Christ;
> You may be filled with the fullness of God.

Thanks be to God, Paul is always faithful to root us in the greatness and grandeur of God. He reminds us that God can do far more than we could ask or think and that all glory belongs to Jesus, in the Church.

## Conclusion

It is good to take time and reflect on the truth that God has established a search-and-rescue mission just for you. Jesus established the Church and commissioned the Apostles to proclaim the Gospel to all corners of the earth. The mystery of the Gospel was once hidden but is now clearly revealed through the Church so that you can boldly put your faith in Christ. All of this was done so that you might be strengthened in your inner man and have the power to live for God in this life, so as to be with Him in the next.

## Study Questions

1. You were once a hostage of sin and death. When were you rescued? When did you climb into the helicopter of God's love (so to speak) and hear the words, "You are free?"

2. Reading a mystery is exciting because you know by the end of the book you will have the answers. Spiritually, you are involved in a great mystery. How grateful are you that the mystery of Christ has been revealed to you?

3. Who are the main people God sent to assist in your rescue?

4. Now that you have been freed, you may want to assist in freeing others. Do you believe God would use you to rescue others? In what way?

# CHAPTER 6

# Walk Your Talk

---

Live a life worthy of Christ and grow into a mature man
EPHESIANS 4:1–16

Smyrna, Roman Empire, AD 155: A young man is brought before the Roman proconsul and forced to his knees. He is visibly afraid and his head is hung low.

"You have news as to the whereabouts of the criminal?" asks the proconsul.

The young man offers a weak "Yes," in reply.

"How do I know your information is accurate?" barks the proconsul.

"If I lie to you, you will kill me," says the young man. "I want to live."

The proconsul quickly summons horsemen and foot soldiers. With swords in hand they swiftly dispatch to capture the rebel. This criminal has eluded them many times before. If it weren't for the young man who betrayed his confidence, the location of the rebel would still be unknown.

The soldiers arrive at the house and barge in to prevent any escape. They head to an upper room to find an elderly man of eighty-six years reclining on a couch.

"Where's Polycarp?" asks the centurion.

"I am he," answers the elderly man.

The soldiers are taken aback that such a show of force was made to apprehend such a frail old man. A centurion informs Polycarp that he is charged with the crime of being a Christian, and that he will be taken immediately to the stadium for trial.

As Polycarp is brought into the stadium he hears a voice from heaven, "Be strong, and show thyself a man, O Polycarp." This strengthens his spirit and prepares him for the trial at hand.

Brought before the proconsul, Polycarp is given this choice: Renounce Christ, proclaim "Caesar is Lord," and live, or confess that he is a Christian and die. Romans considered Christians to be atheists because Christians believe in only one God and none of the many Roman gods.

"Have respect for your old age," says the proconsul, "and swear that Caesar is Lord, and you will go free. Renounce Christ and say of the Christians, 'Away with the atheists!'"

Polycarp knows this is his moment of truth. He was personally taught by the Apostle John and has been preaching Christ throughout the Roman Empire. He is bishop of Smyrna and revered by the entire Catholic Church. If he chooses to reject Christ now, he rejects the God who saves him. Polycarp can invalidate a lifetime of service in an instant. The invitation to walk his talk has never been so clear or challenging.

Instead of renouncing Christ, Polycarp fixes his gaze upon the proconsul and declares, "Eighty-six years have I served Christ and He never did me any injury. How then can I blaspheme my King and my Savior?"

He then turns to the pagan masses in the stadium. With a stern look on his face he groans and waives his hand at them saying, "Away with the atheists!" This angers the crowd and enrages the proconsul.

"I have wild beasts that will tear you to shreds unless you repent," says the proconsul.

"Call for them," replies Polycarp. "We are not accustomed to repent of what is good in order to adopt that which is evil."

"I will burn you with fire if you do not repent," says the proconsul.

"You threaten me with fire which burns for only an hour," replies Polycarp, "but you are ignorant of the fire of the coming judgment and of eternal punishment, reserved for the ungodly. Why do you wait? Do to me what you will."

The more Polycarp speaks, the greater his joy and the proconsul's rage become. The proconsul sends a messenger into the stadium to proclaim three times, "Polycarp has declared himself a Christian!" Immediately, the massive crowd cries out in uncontrollable fury and clamors for Polycarp to be burned at the stake.

In stark contrast, Polycarp shows a great peace as he is brought to the floor of the stadium. He tells the executioners that it is not necessary to nail him to the stake, as is the custom, but that God will give him the grace to stand in the fire.

Polycarp's earthly life ended in the confidence of knowing that heaven is his true home. As he had done throughout his life, Polycarp lived in his actions that which he boldly professed with his lips.

### Baby Steps

Up until now, we've been taking small steps as Paul has laid the foundation of our spiritual reality as Christians:

1. We are chosen in Christ to be sons of God and full heirs to His kingdom.
2. God desires us to know and understand the Christian faith and the power of our hope in Christ.
3. We were once dead in our sin, but God made us alive through Christ by a free gift of grace, and He called us to obedience.
4. Through the Cross of Christ we can now have peace between men, and between mankind and God.
5. God has been personally searching for you and has revealed the mystery of the Gospel— namely, that all people have access to God through Jesus Christ.

The things listed above ground us in the spiritual reality that has taken place in us through faith and Baptism. Understanding this big picture is essential for allowing us to take the next step—actively living for Christ. Pope St. John Paul II explicitly connected understanding our faith as a prerequisite to living our faith. He said, "Firm, well-thought-out convictions lead to courageous and upright actions."[1] You are called to live courageously for Christ. In the rest of Ephesians, Paul shifts gears and begins to help us understand how to courageously walk our talk.

### Walk This Way | Verse 1

**"I THEREFORE, A PRISONER FOR THE LORD, BEG YOU TO WALK IN A MANNER WORTHY OF THE CALLING TO WHICH YOU HAVE BEEN CALLED"**

"Do as I say, not as I do!" Has this ever slipped out of your mouth when talking to your family, friends, or coworkers? Probably not. Most of us are disciplined enough not to actually say the words, but the equivalent may have been sufficiently said through our actions. You might tell the kids to stop yelling by yelling at them; tell your wife to stop nagging while you start pointless arguments; tell your coworkers to be more efficient while you spend your time "looking busy" instead of being busy; decry excessive sexuality in our culture, but take a second look at a provocatively dressed woman.

Knowing our propensity to simply talk a good game, Paul gives us this charge:

"Walk in a manner worthy of your calling!"

To what have you been called? Royal sonship. You are a son of God, chosen by grace to live for Christ, and your life should show it. In essence, Paul is throwing down the challenge: Walk your talk! "Do as I say and not as I do" is not compatible with the Christian life. Jesus said, "If any man would come after me, let him deny himself and take up his cross and follow me" (Mt 16:24). Jesus is the ultimate example of walking the talk and He asks us to follow

---

1. Pope John Paul II, Apostolic Exhortation On Catechesis in Our Time *Catechesi Tradendae* (October 16, 1979), 22.

His lead. Jesus never asks us to do anything that He has not already done.

## Power Walking | Verses 2–3

**"WITH ALL LOWLINESS AND MEEKNESS, WITH PATIENCE, FORBEARING ONE TO ANOTHER IN LOVE, EAGER TO MAINTAIN THE UNITY OF THE SPIRIT IN THE BOND OF PEACE."**

After Paul calls us to walk our talk, he gives us six words that should describe our walk (how we live): lowliness, meekness, patience, forbearing, unity, and peace. Because men are drawn to power and strength, we often don't do well with biblical words that sound weak. At first reading, these don't seem to be power words. You probably didn't get up this morning and say, "Man, I want to be lowly today!" Most men look at these descriptive words of the Christian life and think, "Doormat!" Let's break down what these words really mean. The New Testament was originally written in Greek, and many times the original Greek word has a much deeper meaning than our English word.

### Lowliness

Lowliness means having a modest, humble opinion of yourself. Any strong leader must know his limits and not succumb to pride. The Catechism says that we wait in anticipation for the return of Jesus "in memory of his first coming in the lowliness of the flesh, and in the hope of his second coming in glory [Cf. *Mk* 13; *Lk* 21:34–36] (CCC 2612)." Jesus was lowly, but Jesus was not weak.

### Meekness

To be meek is to have a mild character and a gentle spirit—specifically, a submissive spirit towards God. Meekness is willingly submitting to God's will, trusting that He knows best (CCC 716).

Jesus said of Himself, "I do nothing on my own authority but speak thus as the Father taught me" (Jn 8:28). Jesus had all authority (Mt 28:18), yet was a man under authority.

## Patience

This word is more familiar, but still needs clarification. To be patient is to endure, to be steadfast, to persevere, and most challenging, to be slow in avenging wrongs. A good physical workout requires endurance and perseverance, and a slow, consistent approach to change. It should be no surprise that our spiritual workout needs the same thing.

## Forbearing

Forbearance pertains to how we interact with others. It means to hold up under pressure and to stand up straight and firm. This is why we are to forebear in love. Paul knows we can respond to another person with exasperation and frustration, but we are called to firmly support others in a loving manner.

## Unity

This familiar word can be watered down to mean working together. While that is certainly a part of unity, the root meaning of this word is really agreement or unanimity (full agreement between two or more people). We are called to full agreement of the Spirit. In the Body of Christ, there are not to be theological lone rangers or cafeteria Catholics. There is one Spirit and we are to be fully united in Him.[2]

---

2. The same Greek word for unity appears again in verse 13, specifically stating that we should have unity (full agreement) of the faith.

## Peace

Finally, peace is what should bond (tie) us together. It is through peace that we pursue the unity previously mentioned. If we are living in peace, we are living in security, safety, and prosperity. Through peace, we can develop a deep trust with others and between God and us.

Nothing in these words suggests that you be a doormat. Each word represents a characteristic found in strong, successful leaders from all walks of life. As we saw with Polycarp, when you seek to live these words, you will be prepared for the toughest decisions in life and to walk in a manner worthy of your calling.

## Walking In Oneness | Verses 4–6

**"THERE IS ONE BODY AND ONE SPIRIT, JUST AS YOU WERE CALLED TO THE ONE HOPE THAT BELONGS TO YOUR CALL, ONE LORD, ONE FAITH, ONE BAPTISM, ONE GOD AND FATHER OF US ALL WHO IS ABOVE ALL AND THROUGH ALL AND IN ALL."**

Paul goes on to say there is one Father, one Spirit, one Lord (Jesus), and one Church, one faith, and one Baptism. This is a simple construction of the source of our faith, the evidence of its unity, means of preservation, and how we enter into it. What is this source? The Trinity: Father, Son, and Holy Spirit (CCC 234). This one faith was revealed by God and entrusted to the Church (body) (1 Cor 12:12–27; Eph 5:23; Col 1:18, 24), which preserves it, and is entered into through faith and Baptism.

The oneness of what we believe is also reflected in the name "Catholic Church." The word "catholic" means universal. The Catholic Church is not a sect, nor is it made up of sects; it is universal and unified in every aspect. This unity is derived from Christ's relationship with His Father; they are one, therefore we are one (Jn 17). While there is great cultural diversity in the Church, on doctrine the Church speaks as with one voice throughout the world.[3] It is not the mark of a Christian to pick and choose which teachings to believe. Jesus gave us a unified whole and we are to receive all that He gives.

## Walking under Authority | Verses 7–12

"BUT GRACE WAS GIVEN TO EACH OF US ACCORDING TO THE MEASURE OF CHRIST'S GIFT. THEREFORE IT IS SAID, 'WHEN HE ASCENDED ON HIGH HE LED A HOST OF CAPTIVES, AND HE GAVE GIFTS TO MEN' . . . AND HIS GIFTS WERE THAT SOME SHOULD BE APOSTLES, SOME PROPHETS, SOME EVANGELISTS, SOME PASTORS AND TEACHERS, TO EQUIP THE SAINTS FOR THE WORK OF MINISTRY, FOR BUILDING UP THE BODY OF CHRIST."

This unity is made possible because God gave us an authority structure. The problem is that we don't like authority. We all want to be master of our own destiny. Without even trying we are prone to accept relativism, believing that no one should tell us what to do. Each person should follow his own path. The problem is, that really doesn't work.

What would driving be like without stoplights? What would a football game be like without a referee? How would a war proceed without generals? How would a business grow if every employee made his own decisions? None of these things would work without well-developed authority structures. If this is true in the secular realm, it must be even truer in the spiritual realm, because we are dealing with eternal results— heaven and hell.

Paul tells us that Christ determined some should be apostles, prophets, evangelists, pastors, and teachers. These all reflect the teaching office of the Church. The local bishop in your diocese is a true successor to the Apostles and carries the full teaching authority for his diocese. The priest and deacon share in this teaching authority (CCC 886, 861–862).

---

3. CCC 173; St. Irenaeus clearly teaches the universal nature of the Church around AD 190.

Their job is "to equip the saints for the work of ministry" and for "building up the body of Christ." Christ gave us bishops, priests, and deacons so we could be taught effectively and authoritatively, but there is a catch. To receive teaching, you must first submit yourself to their authority. It is incumbent upon the bishops, priests, and deacons to teach the truth and it is incumbent on us to follow their teaching. Any layperson who teaches does so in submission to the hierarchy. Would it make sense for God to establish authority in secular institutions (like business and the military) but allow His own Church to be every man for himself?

## Walk like a Man | Verse 13

**"UNTIL WE ALL ATTAIN TO THE UNITY OF THE FAITH AND OF THE KNOWLEDGE OF THE SON OF GOD, TO MATURE MANHOOD, TO THE MEASURE OF THE STATURE OF THE FULLNESS OF CHRIST;"**

God gave us the teaching authority of the Church for a number of reasons, not the least of which is to help us become fully men. What does it mean to be a man? There have been many cultural definitions over the years. Many of them involve showing strength, toughness, or sexual virility. Paul indicates that the key to maturing as a man is to be united in our Christian faith to the teaching authority of the Church.

The word "unite" used in verse thirteen is the same word used in verse two, which means agreement or unanimity (full agreement between two or more people). Part of what is needed to be a mature man is full agreement with the teaching authority established by Jesus. When the pope speaks or the bishops teach, we should listen and follow their lead. Why? Because Christ is the key to everything. The more we are perfectly united to the teaching of Christ, the more success and satisfaction we will have in life—in marriage, relationships, career, money, recreation, family, children, sexual relations, and more. Since God is the giver of these gifts, the more we know Him, the more effective we will be at properly managing those gifts. In other words, drawing closer to God gives us a better understanding of His plan for us and the wisdom in knowing how we can best use the gifts He has given us.

Paul goes on to say that Christ is the standard by which we are measured. "I don't need to go to confession, I'm not a jerk like so and so over there who drinks too much and kicks his dog." Jesus Christ was the ultimate man, and the more we seek the fullness of Christ the more manly we become. No matter what the subject, it always comes back to Jesus Christ.

## Grow Up | Verses 14–16

"SO THAT WE MAY NO LONGER BE CHILDREN, TOSSED BACK AND FORTH AND CARRIED ABOUT WITH EVERY WIND OF DOCTRINE, BY THE CUNNING OF MEN, BY THEIR CRAFTINESS IN DECEITFUL WILES. RATHER, SPEAKING THE TRUTH IN LOVE, WE ARE TO GROW UP IN EVERY WAY INTO HIM WHO IS THE HEAD, INTO CHRIST, FROM WHOM THE WHOLE BODY, JOINED AND KNIT TOGETHER BY EVERY JOINT WITH WHICH IT IS SUPPLIED, WHEN EACH PART IS WORKING PROPERLY, MAKES BODILY GROWTH AND UPBUILDS ITSELF IN LOVE."

Has your wife (or a female friend if you're not married) ever said to you, "When will you grow up?" This statement usually follows some random act on your part that a woman would never consider doing. You might have played a stupid joke on your wife; decided to take the all-wheel drive minivan for doughnuts in the mud; taught your kids how to burp the alphabet; or done some stupid display of male aggression that ends up with your blood on the outside of your skin. You look at yourself and say, "Victory!" Your wife just shakes her head and gives you one of "those looks."

Paul is giving us one of those, "It's time to grow up" talks. The further result of being submitted to the teaching authority of the Church is that we will stop being spiritual children and grow up into "another Christ." Once we have been "equipped" through the teaching of the Church, we will no longer be "tossed back and forth" by every wind of doctrine. Being rooted in Christ, through the teaching of the Church, is like holding on to a huge anchor that will never move. Those who are not anchored in the authority of the Church are constantly put on the ropes by our ever-changing culture.

Many of our non-Catholic brothers and sisters in Christ truly love Jesus, but are constantly blown by "every wind of doctrine" as new teachers arrive with novel teachings. If one is not anchored to the unchanging truth of Christ in the Church (Heb 13:8; 1 Tim 3:15; Mt 16:18), there is no baseline by which to determine what is true, and everything is left to private opinion and private interpretation of Scripture.

Finally, Paul reminds us that Christ is the head and we are His body. That means Christ calls the shots and we follow. The head is the one that controls the limbs, not the other way around. We must never shy away from the full truth of the Gospel, but as always, love must be our guide. Without love we will simply become obnoxious (1 Cor 13:1).

## Conclusion

Once we understand who we are in Jesus, we are to live for Jesus. We should not be men who look like heaven on Sunday and live like hell on Monday. If our actions do not match our words, we will become discredited witnesses to our children, spouse, friends, and to God. At Mass, we profess what we believe in the Nicene Creed. We don't make that profession just to fill time, but it is a statement of what we profess to believe and therefore what we profess to live.

Thankfully, God has given us the Church to teach the Gospel of Jesus Christ with clarity and authority so that we can become mature men, leaving indecisive childishness behind and growing up into the fullness of Christ—the head of the Church. May we grow in strength through the Holy Spirit, and if we are challenged to deny our faith in word or deed,[4] may we be able to say like Polycarp, "For

---

4. This could come in many forms: sexual temptation; impure movies, music, television, video games; peer pressure from friends or family, etc. Rarely are we met with an overt appeal to reject our Christian faith.

years have I served Christ and He never did me any injury. How then can I blaspheme my King and my Savior?"

## Study Questions

1. Have you ever had people question or ridicule your faith in God? What happened?

2. Are there specific areas in your life where your actions and words don't match up with what you believe? Give an example.

3. Reading the meaning of the six words Paul uses to describe our Christian walk, can you see how these are words of strength and not weakness? Explain.

4. What would you say is one thing required to truly submit to someone else?

5. The more we seek the fullness of Christ, the more manly we become. Give an example of how this can be true.

6. As you look back at your life, can you see specific areas where you have "grown up?" Can you see areas where your faith has matured you and changed you? Give an example.

# CHAPTER 7

# An Exercise in Futility

Without Christ, you will constantly strive and never be satisfied

EPHESIANS 4:17–32

During the mid-1800s, the Wild West was home to endless adventure. It was a place where dreams came true for those tough enough to survive. The gold rush in California brought adventure seekers from every walk of life to the Golden State. Toward the latter part of the 1800s came the taming of the Northwest. A growing logging industry brought people to the evergreen state and the city of Seattle was born. Seattle is now a beautiful city, but at that time it was possibly the worst planned city in the United States.

Of all the possible locations, the founders chose to build the city on tidelands. Part of the bay was filled in to make an artificial peninsula stable enough for construction and high enough to keep buildings above the tides, which seemed a good idea at first.

With the city essentially being built on a marsh near sea level, heavy rains and regular flooding made the roads extremely muddy. Horse-drawn wagons became mired and large holes made navigation a chore. At one time, the local paper ran a story of a boy who drowned in a pothole that was eleven feet wide and six feet deep.

The challenges didn't cease upon entering a building. Like many cities of the day, sewer systems and indoor plumbing were becoming popular, and being near the bay made disposing of city sewage very easy—just run the sewer pipes into the bay. But the good intentions of the city planners once again fell short.

Every person living in Seattle knew the tides, and tide charts were published daily in the paper. The reason? One never wanted to be caught on the toilet at high tide. Since the city was nearly at sea level, toilets were notorious outlets for the sewer backflow that occurred at high tide. Uninformed newcomers would be called "wetbacks" until they learned which toilets erupted in fountains.

One attempted solution was to elevate the toilets, but elevating a toilet a foot or two wouldn't do. Many toilets were elevated anywhere from six to nearly eighteen feet. When nature called, men and women had to exercise great patience as they climbed a ladder or very precarious stairs.

While these issues were problematic, they do not compare to the move made by city planners after the great fire of 1889. Thirty-three city blocks were completely destroyed by fire and presented a golden opportunity to raise the height of the city as they rebuilt (which would solve the sewage issue). But there was a problem.

The city owned the streets and the businesses owned the property under their buildings. The business owners were not ready to raise the level of their properties, but the city insisted on moving forward with raising the streets. What resulted was a waffle-like downtown. The streets were raised anywhere from twelve to thirty feet, while the businesses remained at their original height. To cross the street, pedestrians literally had to ascend a ladder on one side and descend a ladder on the other. This was a safety nightmare as pedestrians and occasionally horses would fall into the walkways below.

Eventually the businessmen came to see that piecemeal measures addressing flooding and sewage problems were an exercise in futility. With some reluctance, and after a bit of time, the businessmen saw the writing on the wall and all added a second story to match the street. Finally, Seattle was flowing freely and, when nature called, no one had to worry about sitting on a geyser if they happened to be without their tide chart.

## Insanity

When someone is using ineffective methods to achieve a desired result we say he's engaged in an "exercise in futility." In life we can try to succeed and constantly be frustrated that our efforts do not seem to work. We need to find different methods. A definition of insanity, widely attributed to Albert Einstein, is doing the same thing over and over again and expecting different results.

How many times have you vowed to change something like your marriage, work habits, parenting, finances, lustful thoughts, language, entertainment, and more, but only have a series of repeated attempts to show for your effort? In this second half of Ephesians 4, Paul gets very specific on why people make bad choices and how they can find victory.

## No God = Know Futility | Verses 17–19

"**Now this I affirm and testify in the Lord, that you must no longer walk as the Gentiles walk, in the futility of their minds; they are darkened in their understanding, alienated from the life of God because of the ignorance that is in them due to their hardness of heart; they have become callous and have given themselves up to licentiousness, greedy to practice every kind of uncleanness.**"

A computer technician was called out to a lady's house to fix her computer. Upon his arrival, she informed him that her mouse pointer was frozen on the screen. She tried everything, even restarting the computer, but nothing worked. The tech looked at the computer for five seconds, and then said, "It's fixed." The woman's surprise changed to exasperation when he informed her that her mouse was unplugged.

Ignorant people lack the understanding necessary to accomplish even basic actions. The computer was an easy fix, but the woman had *no* technical understanding. To her, an unplugged mouse was no different from a broken motherboard. All she knew was that the computer didn't work.

Paul strongly urges us not to walk as the Gentiles. Why? Because those without Christ will only arrive at flawed answers to life's biggest issues. Paul breaks it down like this:

> Gentiles are hardened toward God;
> This leads to ignorance about God;
> Remaining in ignorance keeps them away from God;
> Without God, they can't understand how to use what God has given;
> Without understanding, the best efforts of their minds can only lead to futile actions.

Paul says that being separated from God makes them "callous" (hard), given to sexual promiscuity, and greedy for impure things.

We don't have to look very far to see these things proved true. Our culture is addicted to sexual and financial excess, and takes pride in its immorality. Our culture says, Instead of fidelity, choose divorce; instead of purity, choose pornography; instead of valuing life, choose abortion; instead of self-restraint, use birth control; instead of financial stewardship, use a credit card; instead of contentment, buy more stuff; instead of meaningful family time, watch TV. Our culture is calling out for meaning, fulfillment, and security, but it is steeped in actions that bring about the exact opposite. A world separated from God can only come to these flawed conclusions; they have no understanding of spiritual things, and the conclusions of their minds lead to futility.

## Teaching Jesus | Verses 20-21

"YOU DID NOT SO LEARN CHRIST!—ASSUMING THAT YOU HAVE HEARD ABOUT HIM AND HAVE BEEN TAUGHT IN HIM, AS THE TRUTH IS IN JESUS."

What is the answer to this dilemma? Jesus. To move from futile actions to fruitful actions, we must be rooted in truth and not opinion. Paul tells us that the truth is *in* Jesus. He doesn't say Jesus leads us to truth, but that Jesus is truth (Jn 14:6). The Christian life is grounded in love and seeks to show love to others (Mk 12:29–31), but this is a spiritual endeavor. If we are not grounded in the source of love, Jesus Christ, we will have actions without substance, which will lead to frustration and burnout. Without love, all good actions in the world are futile (1 Cor 13:1–13).

Paul is saying that you cannot simply stumble upon Jesus, you must actually be taught. You must seek out Christ, as you are doing with this Bible study, and submit yourself to the teaching of His Church. The more you learn, the more you will be able to replace your darkened understanding with enlightened understanding. This process of learning never stops. Even after becoming a Christian through faith and Baptism, if we do not stay close to Jesus we can fall away from God and become ensnared by the traps of Satan.

### Out with the Old and in with the New | Verses 22–24

"**PUT OFF THE OLD MAN WHICH BELONGS TO YOUR FORMER MANNER OF LIFE AND IS CORRUPT THROUGH DECEITFUL LUSTS, AND BE RENEWED IN THE SPIRIT OF YOUR MINDS, AND PUT ON THE NEW MAN, CREATED AFTER THE LIKENESS OF GOD IN TRUE RIGHTEOUSNESS AND HOLINESS.**"

So, how do we go about rejecting the futile and embracing the fruitful? Two things are necessary. The first is to get rid of the "old man." The old man represents your previous life of sin and the things currently entangling you. Get rid of everything that draws you away from God. David said in the Book of Psalms,

> I will walk with integrity of heart
>     within my house;
> I will not set before my eyes
>     anything that is base [worthless].
> (Ps 101:2b, 3a)

Guard your home and reclaim it for Christ. Regulate the TV,

don't watch movies that violate your Christian faith, change the radio station, don't get the Sports Illustrated swimsuit issue, and move the computer to a public place so that you can't surf the web in private. As David did, make a vow before God not to set anything worthless before your eyes and your family's eyes.

The second step is to put on the "new man." The new man is rooted in Christ, reflecting the likeness of God. As the old saying goes, nature abhors a vacuum. Our spiritual life is no different. Once you purge the unjust things from your life, you need to replace them with things that feed your spirit. Paul calls this renewing your mind (Rom 12:2). You literally need to change the way you think. If you do not fill the sinless void with the riches of Christ, the sinful habits will return (see Mt 12:43–45; Lk 11:24–26). Read Scripture and spiritual writings (lives of the saints, apologetics, theology), pray, watch good media, get spiritual reading, join a study group, start a study group, and most of all, make use of God's greatest gift, the sacraments. Each sacrament is a personal encounter with Jesus Christ. Make regular use of Confession, and prepare you and your family well to go to Mass so that you will receive all that God has for you.[1]

### Living the life | Verses 25–30

Just in case we needed more clarity on exactly how our "new man" should be living the Christian life, Paul gives us a straightforward breakdown of things to do and not to do. As we saw in Ephesians 2:10, God has prepared us for good works. The Christian life is to be *lived*, not just believed. While good works are necessary, we must never slip into the mindset that God has a works quota where unless you "do enough" you cannot get to heaven (CCC 162, 2001, 2005).

---

1. An easy family activity to prepare for Mass is to read through the Scripture readings as a family before going to Mass. This greatly helps you to receive Christ through the Scriptures and prepares you to receive Him in the Eucharist.

## Speak the Truth | Verse 25

"THEREFORE, PUTTING AWAY FALSEHOOD, LET EVERY ONE SPEAK THE TRUTH WITH HIS NEIGHBOR, FOR WE ARE MEMBERS ONE OF ANOTHER."

Paul says to speak the truth instead of falsehood. Since we are all a part of one body, what you do affects others in the Body of Christ (1 Cor 12:12–27). When you are with other men, stand up for the truth. Don't succumb to conversations that are contrar y to your faith. When you break God's commands you not only affect yourself, but also everyone connected to you.

## Anger Management | Verse 26

"BE ANGRY BUT DO NOT SIN; DO NOT LET THE SUN GO DOWN ON YOUR ANGER"

It is interesting to see that a person can be angry and not sin. In fact, even God is said to be angry at times (see Ex 34:6; Num 22:22). Within our anger we are given two stipulations: Do not let anger get out of hand and become sin, and do not let the sun go down on our anger (that is, don't hold a grudge). It is okay to be angry at sin, but our response should always be love (Rom 13:8).

## Intruder Alert! | Verse 27

"GIVE NO OPPORTUNITY TO THE DEVIL."

This one is pretty straightforward: Don't help the devil tempt you. To be sure, temptation will find you, but don't help Satan by seeking temptation. Satan will take every opportunity to cause you to sin, therefore you must be on the lookout. In other words, it is one thing for a postman to be chased and bitten by a dog when going about his route, but woe be to the postman who seeks out the dog. The second part of an act of contrition says, "I firmly intend, with your help, to do penance, sin no more, and to *avoid whatever leads me to sin*." That is the key. Identify what leads you into sin and stay as far away as possible.

## Work Hard, Be Generous | Verse 28

**"Let the thief no longer steal, but rather let him labor, doing honest work with his hands, so that he may be able to give to those in need."**

Be a hard worker and a man of integrity. Most people probably don't steal from the mall, but do you take advantage of the supplies at work? Have you ever copied CDs and given them to friends? Have you ever cheated on your taxes? Stealing is stealing, period. God calls you to work hard and be generous to those in need. (This includes tithing to the Church.)

## Speak Up to Build Up | Verse 29

**"Let no evil talk come out of your mouths, but only such as is good for edifying, as fits the occasion, that it may impart grace to those who hear."**

Ephesians 4:29 is a verse everyone should memorize, especially those who have difficulty with a foul or critical mouth. Many times people only focus on eliminating swearing, but leave in demeaning or offensive language. Paul says let "no evil talk" come out of your mouth. Our conversations should build others up and impart to them the grace of God.

## Offending the Holy Spirit | Verse 30

**"And do not grieve the Holy Spirit of God, in whom you were sealed for the day of redemption."**

The Holy Spirit is the third Person of the Blessed Trinity. This verse helps us understand that the Holy Spirit is actually a Person and not a force. A force cannot be grieved, but a person can. The Holy Spirit is grieved when we sin. Remember in Ephesians 1:13, 14, Paul says the Holy Spirit is the guarantee of our inheritance, of our salvation in Jesus. When we sin we are offending the Holy Spirit in us, who is preserving us for the day of salvation.

## Opposites Attract | Verses 31-32

"**LET ALL BITTERNESS AND WRATH AND ANGER AND CLAMOR AND SLANDER BE PUT AWAY FROM YOU, WITH ALL MALICE, AND BE KIND TO ONE ANOTHER, TENDERHEARTED, FORGIVING ONE ANOTHER, AS GOD IN CHRIST FORGAVE YOU.**"

Have you ever called a customer's service line and asked a question, only to be met with a hostile representative who makes you feel like you've interrupted her day by calling? Or have you ever made a genuine mistake while driving, only to have someone yell at you and give you the one finger wave—as if they had never made a driving mistake in their life? What really throws these people off is when you speak kindly or genuinely smile and wave.

We should treat others with an attitude that reflects Jesus Christ. Paul wraps up this section with a list of attitudes that we should not have and a list that we should have. The latter seems to be the remedy to the former. We should not show bitterness, wrath, anger, shouting, slander, and malice. Those hostile passions start from a judgmental place and not a place of love. Wrath mentioned here could be described as volatile anger: anger that happens quickly and then subsides (a real hot-head).

What is the antidote? To others we should be kind, tender-hearted, and forgiving. Those are starting to sound like doormat words again. But before anyone can start complaining, Paul gently reminds us that God has already forgiven us in Christ and that we should extend to others what we have freely received. It is a grave injustice to deny to others what we seek for ourselves.

We are not called to fight fire with fire. We are called to be countercultural and live as Jesus lived. How did Jesus live? He conquered sin through love.

## Conclusion

If you feel like you have tried over and over to fix things in your life without success, turn to Jesus, the Author of life (Acts 3:15), and trade in your futile exercises for fruitful exercises. Don't wait to see if you'll be blown off the toilet. Construct a new building, built on the rock of Jesus Christ.

Since Jesus is the Author of life, He is the one who knows how to live this life and get us safely to the next. We need to be taught the truth, and we need to intentionally seek out the sources of sin and replace them with spiritual resources (especially the sacraments) so that our mind and spirit will be renewed. As we are renewed, the Holy Spirit will help us live for Christ every day as we slowly transform our way of thinking and learn how to give to others what we have freely received in Christ.

## Study Questions

1. Change: We all want it, yet precious few of us seem to *do* it. In what area of your life would you like to see change the most? Be specific.

2. Before you came to know God, what were the areas in which you exercised futility?

3. What are some of the traps Satan uses to ensnare you in sin?

4. Which do you think is more difficult: to get rid of the old man, or to put on the new man? Do you think one affects the other? How?

5. Since the Christian life is to be lived, not just believed, what good works are you involved in? What good works would you like to be involved in?

6. If opposites attract, what are the opposites of anger, cursing, or stealing?

# CHAPTER 8

# Imitation Is the Sincerest Form of Flattery

---

Imitate Christ: Walk in the light and not in sin
EPHESIANS 5:1–20

It is hard to imagine life outside our own cultural context. This is not unique to our day, but natural to men of every age. The stories of history seem but vague memories of a distant time, long forgotten.

In the United States, we worship, buy and sell property, start businesses, create, invent, write, publish, and cross borders as we please. We are a free people in every sense of the word—free to succeed, free to fail, free to be average. But, in the not too distant past, the life we take for granted did not exist here or anywhere else in the world. Kings, queens, emperors, and dictators wielded authority and manipulated the masses at will. They controlled the press, law, property, money, commerce, food, and in many cases, religion. The idea of a government of the people, by the people, and for the people was unheard of. Yet, as history would record, the norms of the past were destined for disuse and gave way to an idea that would truly inspire the imitation of the world.

After Columbus accidentally discovered the "new world" in 1492, interest in immigration to the Americas was steady. The first English settlement was successfully established in Jamestown in 1607, and by 1733 Georgia had become the last of the original thirteen colonies. Each colony had its own local government but was still ultimately ruled by the British parliament.

Around 1765, Parliament began to levy heavy taxes on the American colonies and yet refused to give them any representation in making laws. The old system of "government at the expense of the people" began to wear thin. After repeated failed attempts to secure representation in Parliament, the colonists mounted a series of protests. The British sent troops to quell the unrest, little knowing that this aggressive response would signal the beginning of the end of British rule in the Americas.

The battles of Lexington and Concord erupted in the spring of 1775, and historians would later call this the beginning of the American Revolutionary War. As the fighting continued, colonial leaders agreed on a course of action that would *literally* change the world. These men resolved to establish a new system of government, based on previous philosophical and governmental principles, which would put the fate of the nation in the hands of the people instead of the hands of a ruling class.

Fifty-six men representing the thirteen colonies agreed to put their lives on the line and declared independence from British rule, in hope of a better future. The following are the second paragraph and the last sentence of the Declaration of Independence.

> IN CONGRESS, JULY 4, 1776
> The unanimous Declaration of the thirteen united States of America,
> We hold these truths to be self-evident, that all men are created equal, that they are endowed by their Creator with certain un-alienable Rights, that among these are Life, Liberty and the pursuit of Happiness. —That to secure these rights, Governments are instituted among Men, deriving their just powers from the consent of the governed. . . .
> And for the support of this Declaration, with a firm reliance on the protection of Divine Providence, we mutually pledge to each other our Lives, our Fortunes, and our sacred Honor.

This declaration did not make the American colonies free. Freedom came seven years later at the end of the war in 1783 after thousands of men gave their lives for a freedom they would never see. Five years after the war, the United States Constitution was drafted and modern democracy was born. This constitution was created specifically to limit the power of government so as to ensure the liberty of all citizens, and it has unleashed a wave of human ingenuity, creativity, and prosperity, unparalleled in human history.

This landmark document has literally inspired imitation by the world. Democratic governments were nonexistent before this time. The U.S. Constitution is the oldest active constitution in the world, but no longer alone in its democracy. More than 40 percent of all countries today are democratic and free. The idea of democracy has gained worldwide acceptance, and nearly all countries in the world are self-described as democratic, even if they are not in reality. That for which fifty-six men freely pledged their lives, fortunes, and sacred honor, has now become the standard by which other nations measure their freedom.

## Imitation Nation

Whether it is systems of government or the latest athlete, imitation is recognition of value in the thing being imitated. Our nation's economy thrives off of the natural desire of people to imitate. People want to be like other people—successful, beautiful, impressive people. Marketers pay big money to have a famous athlete or celebrity "endorse" their product or even be seen using their product.

When we break it down, most of our cultural imitation is driven by a desire to look better, feel better, fit in, and be accepted. Most of our imitation comes from external pressure to conform to the standards of our culture: job, car, sports, money, appearance, physique, and so on. In this next section of Ephesians, the Apostle Paul calls us to an imitation that doesn't just make us *feel better*, but actually makes us *be better*. You can lace up Air Jordan shoes all day long, but if you have a lousy jump shot, the shoes won't change a thing. Imitating Jordan by wearing his shoes is merely superficial. Paul invites us to practice a much deeper imitation, an imitation where the one doing the imitating is transformed by the One being imitated. Spiritually speaking, you really do get a better jump shot with this imitation.

## Imitate Perfection | Verses 1-2

"**Therefore be imitators of God, as beloved children. And walk in love, as Christ loved us and gave himself up for us, a fragrant offering and sacrifice to God.**"

Why has Paul worked so hard to teach us about our true identity in Christ in the first part of Ephesians? Paul has laid this foundation because he now unfolds our greatest challenge and ultimate purpose: Imitate God, in the person of Jesus Christ. Paul knows that if we try to live the Christian life on our own strength, we will fail. Our only hope is to be rooted in Christ, filled with His grace, and living our lives by the power of the Holy Spirit. The Christian life is impossible outside of Christ. While this might sound obvious, countless men try to imitate the Christian life without truly knowing Christ. We are called to imitate Christ, not the Christian life.

Here is the distinction: To imitate the Christian life, one focuses on a set of quantifiable actions, based on do's and don'ts, to try and *look like* a Christian. That is an external approach based on our own works, which breeds failure. To imitate Christ, one focuses on a person (Jesus), through whom comes internal renewal, which causes one *to be* a Christian. That is a spiritual approach based on grace, empowered by the Holy Spirit, and brings lasting change. The Catechism affirms this truth when it speaks about the challenges of living out the high calling in the Lord's Prayer.

> It is impossible to keep the Lord's commandment by imitating the divine model from outside; there has to be a vital participation, coming from

the depths of the heart, in the holiness and the
mercy and the love of our God. Only the Spirit
by whom we live can make "ours" the same mind
that was in Christ Jesus. (2842)

If you do not have a genuine relationship with Jesus Christ,
you will not be able to live for Jesus. If you do not live for Jesus,
you will find living the Christian life frustrating, in much the same
way as you would find it frustrating to use woodworking tools to fix
the car. For example, if your marriage needs help, knowing Christ
is the first step to setting your marriage straight. Since God is the
author of marriage, getting to know Him is the best way to have a
great marriage.

Imitating Jesus means living a life for Jesus, and there is no
better model than Jesus Himself. The Catechism says,

In all of his life Jesus presents himself as *our
model*. He is "the perfect man" [*GS* 38; cf. *Rom
1* 5:5; *Phil* 2:5], who invites us to become his
disciples and follow him. In humbling himself,
*he has given us an example to imitate*, through his
prayer he draws us to pray, and by his poverty
he calls us to accept freely the privation and
persecutions that may come our way. (520,
emphasis added)

The question you must ask yourself is whether you are truly
ready to follow Jesus, to "freely" say no to sin and say yes to the
persecutions that come with discipleship. Living for Jesus brings
the greatest fulfillment possible, but we live in a world that does not
accept Jesus. Living for Christ is countercultural.

## Imitate Purity: Mind, Mouth, Action | Verses 3-4

**"BUT IMMORALITY AND ALL IMPURITY OR COVETOUSNESS MUST NOT EVEN BE NAMED AMONG YOU, AS IS FITTING AMONG SAINTS. LET THERE BE NO FILTHINESS, NOR SILLY TALK, NOR LEVITY, WHICH ARE NOT FITTING; BUT INSTEAD LET THERE BE THANKSGIVING."**

The moment a man decides to actively live for Jesus, he will surely be met with temptations. Satan knows that discouragement is his greatest weapon. Knowing our weaknesses, Paul doesn't waste any time hitting us between the eyes and getting our attention. He calls us into account in two areas: sexual sin, and vulgar, demeaning talk. Paul doesn't say that we should just do our best, but that there should be *none* of this sin in our life.

### Sexual Purity

God made men to be sexually attracted to women and therefore the desire is good, but the only context for sexual expression is within marriage. All men, married or not, are called to live chaste lives. Sexual lust, masturbation, pornography, sexual expression outside of marriage, and all homosexual acts are grave sins and have no place in the life of a Christian man (CCC 2337–59). There is no circumstance or state in life where these acts can be justified on the grounds of relief or unfulfillment.

As Paul says, these should not even be mentioned among Christians. This goes for the media you choose to read and watch. Get rid of anything sexually suggestive, and don't limit "sexually suggestive" to that which is explicitly pornographic. Eliminate everything that is contrary to God. Any sexual advance or sexual expression outside of the context of marriage is sin, including commercials, cheerleaders, primetime TV shows, men's magazines, and the like. None of these media are intrinsically evil by themselves, but when they are used for sexual effect—excitement, arousal, titillation, stimulation, shock—they become a near occasion of sin[1] that can easily lead to actual sin.

---

1. An occasion of sin is any person, place, or thing that can be a reason, cause, or

## Purity in Conversation

It is all too easy to be with the guys and allow yourself to go along with a conversation that dishonors God, women, and your fellow man. Our mouths are the gateway to action: Where your mouth goes, so will your body (Jas 3:1–12). The first step to purifying your actions is to purify your mouth. Paul is not saying that joking around and innocent fun are wrong. He is saying that any conversation that is obscene, godless, or making fun at the expense of another person (where it becomes offensive) is not acceptable.

Our speech should be such that anyone could listen to our conversations. We should not have a "Sunday" vocabulary and a "Monday" vocabulary, but a manner of speech that honors God at every turn. Paul roots this type of conversation in thankfulness. When we are thankful for our wife, family, job, and material possessions, our conversation will naturally take a more positive tone. A good question to ask yourself is, "Would people know that I am a Christian by my conversations throughout the day?"

## An Eternal Decision | Verses 5–6

**"BE SURE OF THIS, THAT NO IMMORAL OR IMPURE MAN, OR ONE WHO IS COVETOUS (THAT IS, AN IDOLATER), HAS ANY INHERITANCE IN THE KINGDOM OF CHRIST AND OF GOD. LET NO ONE DECEIVE YOU WITH EMPTY WORDS, FOR IT IS BECAUSE OF THESE THINGS THAT THE WRATH OF GOD COMES UPON THE SONS OF DISOBEDIENCE."**

Do hypocritical politicians bother you? You know the type. The kind of politician that will say anything to get a vote, but once in office, takes the easy road when push comes to shove. This kind of person is frustrating because he says one thing and does another. This might work in politics, but Paul makes it clear it does not work for the Christian life.

Paul says we cannot receive our inheritance in God's kingdom

---

circumstance for someone to sin. The higher the risk, the more proximate or "near" the occasion is said to be.

if we are the immoral, impure, and covetous person from verse three. We cannot freely receive God's saving grace and at the same time willfully live like sinners. The two do not mix. To consider masturbation, pornography, or sexual relations outside of marriage compatible with the Christian life would be like your wife telling you that she's committed to you forever, but she's going to be intimate with other men whenever she wants. Her actions would negate her words. You can't get to heaven by living like hell. Eternity is at stake and we must not diminish this reality.

Now, Paul is not talking about the Christian man that desires Christ, but struggles with sin from time to time. God knows we will sin and that is why He gave us the Sacrament of Penance.[2] Anytime we seriously sin, we should fall on our knees and make a sincere act of contrition, right then and there. Then, if we are dealing with grave matter, get to Confession as soon as possible. God's grace and freedom in the Sacrament of Penance is powerful. Satan's best tool is to keep you in fear and thinking it is best if no one knows your sin. The reality is that God already knows your sin and He's just waiting for you to acknowledge it.

## Get New Friends | Verse 7

### "THEREFORE DO NOT ASSOCIATE WITH THEM"

At the close of verse six, Paul refers to those steeped in sin as the "sons of disobedience." Paul then says simply and forcefully, "do not associate with them." Living a successful Christian life is not rocket science. One of the easiest things we can do is identify the people and places that can lead us into sin, and cease to associate with them. Paul tells the Church at Corinth, "Do not be deceived: 'Bad company ruins good morals'" (1 Cor 15:33). Don't pretend to be stronger than you are. To the extent that it is possible, choose your friends wisely.

---

2. Jn 20:21–23; CCC 1440–60 on Penance; CCC 1854–64 on mortal sin.

## Walk in the Light | Verses 8–16

You know what it's like to be home at night when the power has gone out. Suddenly, you are left to navigate in the dark before you can find candles or flashlights, and you trip over things and bump into things. Coming to know Jesus Christ is like turning on the light switch of life. Suddenly you can see all of the stumbling blocks and avoid them.

Paul says we are to walk as children of the light and have nothing to do with the unfruitful works of darkness. This exhortation implies that there will be some pain; if one is not acclimated to the light, it will feel uncomfortable at first. Think about what it is like when someone turns on the light while you are sleeping in the middle of the night. The light hurts your eyes, it is difficult to see, and can be a bit disorienting at first. When you begin to walk in the light of Christ, it might be difficult or uncomfortable at first, as old habits die hard and it takes time for our "old man" to be completely replaced by the "new man." Growing spiritually can often feel like the beginning of a weightlifting workout where your muscles feel extra sore as they adjust to the training routine, but if you persevere, you will see a genuine transformation.

Once again, we are implored to have nothing to do with sin, but to expose it. In fact, Paul says we shouldn't even mention the practices of the sinful, but instead learn what pleases God. Lastly, Paul gives us a warning to walk as wise men because the days are evil. We can never let our guard down, because Satan will take advantage of us the moment we do.

## Desire God More Than Beer | Verses 17–20

Imagine that one day you find a lamp and you release a genie from within and he grants you, not three wishes, but a choice: You could have a lifetime supply of beer, or perfect spiritual insight. Which would you choose? Would you have to think it over? The question is, "What do you desire more than God?" The object of desire is likely to be different from one person to the next: money, sex, power, alcohol, acceptance [insert your weakness here]. But Paul specifically puts his finger on alcohol because he knows we might use alcohol to alter our perception of reality when times are tough or when we want to celebrate. Paul calls us to be filled with the Spirit of God rather than alcohol because he knows that only God can truly fulfill us and make us happy. And he knows that when we drink too much we are much more prone to sin.

In all of this he calls us back to the importance of understanding God's will. Nothing replaces understanding our Christian faith, which is the beginning of courageous action. Paul closes by saying that our prayers and songs and all things should be wrapped in thanksgiving. The moment we cease to be thankful is the moment we begin to drift away from God (Rom 1:21–23). The object of our thankfulness should not be vague but firmly rooted in Jesus Christ and directed toward the Father, from whom we will receive our eternal inheritance as sons.

## Conclusion

While the Christian faith can bring the greatest peace and purpose this side of heaven, it is also challenging. The great Catholic author G. K. Chesterton said of Christianity, "The Christian faith has not been tried and found wanting. It has rather been found difficult and left untried." God calls us to a high standard—perfection. Thankfully, God did not leave it for us to decide on what perfection looks like. He sent His Son Jesus to be our model and example (CCC 457–60).

As Christian men, we are to be those who live in the light, with our actions freely visible to all who care to look. We are to imitate Jesus in thought, word, and deed, but our imitation is not to be in the sense of a fake imitation (like imitation leather or diamonds). It is to be in the sense of trying to become like what we imitate. Similar to the countries that have paid the price to imitate the United States and its government of the people, by the people, and for the people, may we seek to imitate Christ and inspire others to do so as well.

## Study Questions

1. Do you have a person in your life that you would like to imitate? What is it you most admire about that individual?

2. Paul calls us to imitate Jesus, not so we will *look* better or *feel* better, but so we can actually *be* better. Name two ways you are now better (more like Jesus) than you once were.

3. Do you think you can live for Jesus without living counter to the culture? How?

4. What is wrong with something being sexually suggestive? If it's just meant to be a funny joke, what is wrong with that?

5. When a person's actions are different from his words, what, in your opinion, is the cause?

6. Have you ever needed to report the wrongdoing of a co-worker or friend? Did you? What happened?

# CHAPTER 9

# No Pain, No Gain

Christ modeled on the Cross what you are to model for your
wife: sacrifice
EPHESIANS 5:21–33

Why do men love sports? We crave the battle. We love the
fight, the pain, and the thrill of victory, even if it's only occasional.
While every sport has its unique intrigue and appeal, baseball is a
magnificent stage where dramatic tension builds like no other. On
October 15, 1988, baseball fans were treated to one of the greatest
dramatic moments in baseball history.

The 1988 World Series showcased two teams. On one hand were
the Oakland Athletics, who strolled in confidently after sweeping
the Boston Red Sox in four games. The A's were the team to beat.
The powerful bats of the "bash brothers," José Canseco and Mark
McGuire, were the admiration of the league, and the pitching staff
led the league in ERA, wins, and saves.

The Dodgers were another matter. They came in as an
underwhelming team in every statistical category, with the
exception of two players: Orel Hershiser, who was nearly invincible
as a pitcher, and the consistent overall performance of league MVP
Kirk Gibson. The contrast of the two teams was even more evident
by the fact that the A's had four regular position players selected for
the All Star team and the Dodgers had none.

With this background, the stage is set.

Prior to game one, the Dodgers receive terrible news. Left fielder Kirk Gibson, the anchor of their team, is out for the game and possibly the entire Series with a severely strained ligament in his right knee. Gibson delivered winning homeruns in games four and five of the Championship Series, and World Series success is highly unlikely without his glove and bat in the game.

The day of game one comes and Gibson awakes early to test the knees. After a few short jogs the excruciating pain makes it clear that he is in no condition to play. At the stadium he takes a golf cart to the training room for treatment and misses the opening introductions because the pain is too intense to walk.

The Dodgers are up by two after the first inning, but the second inning brings a crushing Canseco grand slam and the outcome of the Series seems clear, if not inevitable. By the fifth inning, Gibson lets his wife know she can go home because there was no way his body will sufficiently recover. The Dodgers score a run in the sixth and enter the bottom of the ninth down by one to the A's, 4–3. With their ace closer, Dennis Eckersley, on the mound, the A's are in the power position.

The bottom of the ninth begins and Eckersley retires the first batter with ease. Earlier, during the top of the ninth, Gibson began to tell himself he could make one plate appearance. He convinced himself that once he stepped out on the field, the chanting of fifty thousand fans would get his adrenaline pumping and he could push through the pain. He heard an announcer point out his absence in the dugout and say that he apparently wouldn't make it out for this game. "Not if I can help it," thought Gibson. Unable to sit out any longer, pain or no pain, Gibson told coach Tommy Lasorda that he could pinch-hit.

Now, in the bottom of ninth, Eckersley strikes out the second batter. Lasorda has Gibson waiting in the tunnel so the A's are unaware that he is available. At bat is a power hitter, Mike Davis, with light-hitting Dave Anderson on deck. Eckersley goes after Davis, but doesn't want to give him a pitch he can tie the game with, and walks him on a 3–1 count. With two outs and one man on,

Anderson returns to the dugout and Gibson shocks the crowd as he hobbles out of the dugout and up to the plate. With the roar of the crowd at a fever pitch, Gibson and Eckersley enter into a duel, man against man—winner takes all.

The first pitch blazes outside and Gibson fouls it off. He reels from the pain, nearly stumbles, but catches himself. Eckersley doesn't let up. Same pitch, same result: 0–2. Eckersley then throws a hard sinker Gibson nubs up the first base line. Gibson has to run, but fortunately the ball rolls foul. Next pitch, Eckersley just misses with a slider. Next pitch, foul. Next pitch, ball. The pain shoots through his legs, but Gibson's will is stronger. Next pitch, foul. Next pitch, ball.

This is one of those moments: two outs, bottom of the ninth, down a run, one man on, and a full count. Gibson steps out of the box and takes a moment to think. He recalls the scouting report. Eckersley likes to throw a 3–2 backdoor slider—the same one he threw on the 0–2 pitch—to left-handed hitters. Gibson readies himself, mentally prepares for the pitch, and chooses to ignore the pain.

Eckersley winds, extends, and . . . throws the slider. The crack of the bat cuts through the roar of the crowd, the ball takes flight and sails over the right field fence.

The Dodgers win the game 5–4 and the World Series 4–1. And though he never saw another at-bat, by pushing through the pain Gibson used this one opportunity to lead his team to the championship.

## The Longing of All Men

Many things could be said about this section of Ephesians, but this chapter will focus on the role of the husband toward his wife in light of Christ's relationship with the Church. This will be applicable to all men, whether single, married, consecrated, or priest.

God created men with a desire for women and hard-wired men with a mission to serve and protect. This trait is one of the great mysteries of humanity, and tales have been written in every age of the exploits of brave men and their efforts to win the love of a woman. You might have your own story of a woman who captured your heart and how you went to great lengths to win her love. Our culture usually signifies this attraction in biological terms, focusing on men's natural desire for contact with women's body parts. But the attraction of men to women transcends biology—it is a natural desire with a supernatural purpose.

### To Serve And Protect

In Genesis, the first book of the Bible, we read about the creation of man and woman and learn something very specific about the role of man. After God creates Adam, he is placed in the garden with a very specific job: to serve and protect. Of Adam's duties in the garden, Genesis 2:15 says, "The LORD God took the man and put him in the garden of Eden to *till* it and *keep* it" [emphasis added].

These two words, "till" and "keep," describe Adam's role in the garden. The Hebrew word for "till" means to work or to serve. This could be the work of a job (like farming), service to another, or even priestly service in the temple. The Hebrew word for "keep" means to observe (as in follow) or to keep watch for the purpose of protecting. This could be the duty of observing commands or keeping a watchful eye for those who would seek to do harm. What is interesting is that Adam is given these commands before the creation of Eve—these commands are a part of his very nature.

So Adam is given his job description and then clearly told where the danger exists and what will happen should he fail to serve and protect. God says he may eat of any tree in the garden, but he should not eat from the tree of the knowledge of good and evil, and the moment he eats from the tree, he will die. Adam's mission is clear: Don't let anyone get to that tree.

## The Perfect Woman

Following this encounter, God sets out to create Eve, Adam's wife. First, God parades all the animals in front of Adam to see if any would be a suitable helper for him, and of course none of them are. This divine drama is for Adam's benefit and not because God really thinks the monkey might fill the bill. When Eve arrives, Adam sees she is a special creation and completely different from every living creature. Upon seeing Eve, Adam proclaims, "This at last is bone of my bone and flesh of my flesh" (Gen 2:23).

God put a longing in Adam that could only be satisfied by Eve. There was no comparison between Eve and all other created things. She was unique. In fact, Adam and Eve were both unique because out of all that God created, only they were made in His image and likeness. You, along with all of humanity, are not the product of random, evolutionary chance. You are a special creation, made in the image and likeness of God, created to desire, serve, and protect a woman, and to love God. These longings are natural to our manhood, and every man tries to fulfill these needs in one way or another. But there is only one way to truly satisfy the longing of our heart— God's way (CCC 2548, 2557; Jn 4:14). This mission requires men to sacrifice and push through the pain to find victory.

## Christ and the Church: The Imitation for All Men

After some introductory comments about the role of wives, Paul makes a clear and profound connection: A husband's love for his wife should be like the love Christ has for the Church. At the beginning of Ephesians 5, Paul tells us to imitate God, and in this section he gives husbands a clear and tangible model for imitation. We do not have to guess how to act.

If you are not married you might think this passage of Paul's letter does not apply to you, but that would be a grave mistake. The call to serve and protect—given to Adam even before Eve was created—is natural to all men, regardless of their marital status. It includes an obligation to be strong in the virtues of courage and generosity, which are necessary for heroic sacrifice.

### Single

If you are single and open to marriage, the principles laid out in this section are the foundation stones for finding the right woman and living a healthy marriage. A marriage pursued with the world's methods will be a relationship based on shallow principles unable to endure the test of time.

### Married

If you are married, Paul is laying out for you the keys to a happy, healthy, lifelong marriage. Adherence to Paul's insight will allow you to enjoy spending time with your wife, will bless you with wholesome sexual relations, and will prepare you to be a godly father. If you base your marriage on the portrayal of cheerleaders at an average NFL game, you will never be satisfied in your marriage.

### Priest or Consecrated

If you are a priest or a member of a religious order, you live out your role as husband directly to the bride of Christ, the Church (CCC 1574). Moreover, while all men share in Christ's priesthood to some extent, the priest uniquely shares in the priestly role of Christ to serve and protect the bride. This is a great sacrifice and one to which the entire Church is indebted. The imitation of Christ is for all men.

### Serve One Another | Verse 21

**"BE SUBJECT TO ONE ANOTHER OUT OF REVERENCE FOR CHRIST."**
Paul begins this section with an exhortation for men and women to be subject to one another. No man has the right to

demand anything from his wife, but each spouse should seek to serve the other. This is what Jesus modeled during His ministry. Even though He was God in the flesh, Jesus said to His disciples, "The Son of man came not to be served but to serve, and to give his life as a ransom for many" (Mt 20:28). Even though Jesus has authority over the Church, He came in a posture of service. This mutual service of spouses is rooted in the truth that both men and women are joint heirs in Christ. One is not better than the other (1 Pet 3:7; CCC 1642).

## Like Jesus, a Man Initiates | Verse 23

### "WIVES, BE SUBJECT TO YOUR HUSBANDS, AS TO THE LORD."

One of the greatest teachings of the Christian faith is that God did not wait for us to approach Him, but He pursued us. Even though we were in sin and were rejecting Him, God sought to restore our relationship by sending His Son as a sacrifice for our sins. To follow the example of Christ with the Church is to initiate and model love so that the bride can respond. Paul clearly shows the initiative of God when He says, "God shows his love for us in that while we were yet sinners Christ died for us" (Rom 5:8; see also 1 Jn 4:10). As a man, you are called to initiate and take the lead in your home in everything: spiritually, financially, socially, sexually, etc.

Paul says a husband is the head of his wife like Christ is the head of the Church, that is, the head initiates and the body responds. You cannot take the position that you are waiting for your wife to get her act together. Your faithfulness to initiate and model sacrificial love will make it possible for her to respond. If Jesus waited to come until we got our act together, He never would have come. This requires sacrifice and maybe some pain, but it will be worth it. No pain, no gain. Anything worth having requires work.

## Like Jesus, a Man Lays Down His Life | Verse 25

### "HUSBANDS, LOVE YOUR WIVES, AS CHRIST LOVED THE CHURCH

**AND GAVE HIMSELF UP FOR HER."**

Of all that Jesus did, the Cross is the most visible and transformative event in His earthly life. Jesus came knowing that He would give His life for His bride, the Church. Looking ahead to His coming crucifixion, Jesus said of His life, "No one takes it from me, but I lay it down of my own accord" (Jn 10:18). The Cross was not a surprise to Jesus, and He joyfully endured the Cross because He knew the outcome would mean salvation for His bride (Heb 12:1–3).

While God calls wives to submit to their husbands, He calls husbands to die for their wives. Through the Cross, Christ took our sin upon Himself so that we could be saved. As a man, you are called to lay down your life for your bride and keep you and her away from sin.

You are the guardian of your home and are not to let any arrows from Satan enter in. Being the protector of the home, it is your duty to see that your TV, music, reading material, internet, video games, and all items are not contrary to the Christian life. This is not done through dictatorial commands (although setting boundaries will be necessary), but through loving, informed, and patient leadership. It is your duty to sacrifice your time so that your family can grow spiritually through family prayer, going to Mass, and reading the Bible. Jesus didn't come to be served, but to serve, and you are to do the same.

Why did Christ lay down His life for the Church? Because He loved her. Your sacrificial acts must be borne out of love and empowered by the Holy Spirit. If they are not, you will be working from your own strength and you will not endure. Marriage is a sacrament, which means that God has given you special grace to fulfill what He asks of you. The greatest thing you can do as a husband is keep your family rooted in prayer, Scripture, and the sacraments. Prayer, reading the Bible, and making Confession and the Mass a priority will do wonders for allowing your family to stand against the schemes of the devil. It also helps to eat dinner as a family, shut off the TV, and play a game or some other activity to build family relationships.

## Like Jesus, a Man Leads His Wife to H...

**"THAT HE MIGHT SANCTIFY HER, HAVING**
**WASHING OF WATER WITH THE WORD, THAT H...**
**CHURCH TO HIMSELF IN SPLENDOR, WITHOUT S...**
**ANY SUCH THING, THAT SHE MIGHT BE HOLY AND ...**

What is your ultimate mission in regard to ...
her to heaven! As was said earlier, God gives us na...
a supernatural purpose. God has not given us a natu...
women to satisfy our own lusts. He has given us the comma...
serve and protect, to give our life on behalf of her so that she will
know God to the fullest extent possible. Following Christ's example,
Paul gives all husbands a high calling: Sanctify your wife (make holy)
and present her to God without spot, wrinkle, or blemish. Paul is
not talking about physical features but spiritual features.

Do your actions draw your wife to holiness? Does your speech
build her up or tear her down? Do you treat her as a sexual object or
as a gift from God? Do you honor her by not viewing sexually explicit
media in private or with her? Do you take the lead in deepening
your spiritual relationship with God? Do you pray for her? Do you
serve her first or demand service first? The main question is: Are
you preparing your wife for heaven?

## Like Jesus, a Man Stays Faithful Forever | Verses 28–31

**"EVEN SO HUSBANDS SHOULD LOVE THEIR WIVES AS THEIR OWN**
**BODIES. HE WHO LOVES HIS WIFE LOVES HIMSELF. FOR NO MAN**
**EVER HATES HIS OWN FLESH, BUT NOURISHES AND CHERISHES IT, AS**
**CHRIST DOES THE CHURCH, BECAUSE WE ARE MEMBERS OF HIS BODY.**
**FOR THIS REASON A MAN SHALL LEAVE HIS FATHER AND MOTHER AND**
**BE JOINED TO HIS WIFE, AND THE TWO SHALL BECOME ONE FLESH."**

With such a high calling, we begin to see why God made marriage
for a lifetime—it takes time to learn how to lead, and eternity is at
stake. Paul wraps up this section by recalling the words from Genesis
2:24 about the first marriage between Adam and Eve, "The two shall
become one flesh." When God brings a man and woman together

ent of Matrimony, they are truly united in one flesh
d one heart. Spiritual death comes when the bonds of
severed. During His earthly ministry, Jesus reaffirmed
rriage is for a lifetime and that divorce plus remarriage (if
s in a valid marriage) creates a state of perpetual adultery.[1]

Again, this union of husband and wife reflects Christ and His
urch. Christ will never leave His Church, because the Church
is His body—He can't leave Himself (Heb 13:5; Mt 28:20, 16:18).
When Paul says to love your wife as your own body, it is because
she has literally become a part of you. You are called to love her
and treat her with reverence and respect because that is what you
would do for yourself. The spiritual union between you and your
wife is unbreakable, just as the biological union is unbreakable
with the conception of a child. There is no way to separate the
biological deposits of a husband and wife in a child, and neither
is there a way to separate a true (valid) spiritual union between a
husband and a wife.

## Conclusion: Informed and Purposeful Sacrifice

Jesus Christ came to suffer and lay down His life for His bride,
and husbands are called to follow Christ's example. The key to
making this level of sacrifice is understanding. Think back to the
opening story about Kirk Gibson. He was able to step up to the
plate and hit the pitch because he knew what was coming—he was
informed. When you are well informed about your Christian faith
and your marriage, you will be able to make courageous, sacrificial
decisions. Pain without purpose breeds hopelessness, but pain with
purpose brings peace. Jesus endured the Cross because of the joy
set before Him. A mother endures labor pain because of the joy of
a baby. A man trains for a sport because of the thrill of victory. A
husband sacrifices for his wife because of the joy of a great marriage
and the coming heavenly reward.

Men do not lay down their lives for valueless things. Pain and

---

1. Matthew 19:3–12, 16–18; Hebrews 13:4; Ephesians 5:3–5; CCC 2384.

suffering are only endured if there is value in the payoff. You must believe your wife is worth fighting for and if you do, push through the pain and prepare her for success in this life and the next.

## Study Questions

1. Are you single but open to marriage? Are you married? Or are you called to the priesthood or consecrated life? Circle one.

2. How can a wife submit to her husband if he is her servant? Shouldn't she be serving him?

3. God calls the husband to lay down his life for his wife. What does that mean to you?

4. What are some practical ways you can begin serving your wife? Consider taking her out, cooking for her, watching the kids, and doing the dishes.

5. Does your marriage include pain or unpleasantness so that, like Jesus, you must endure suffering? Can you also have hope that your sacrifice will bring ultimate salvation and blessings to your wife? How?

6. You are called to keep you and your wife away from sin. Has there been any area where you have led your wife *into* sin? How?

7. You are called to lead in the home by making courageous, sacrificial decisions. Did you realize that this results in eternal rewards? How?

# CHAPTER 10

# Lead by Example

Christian manhood in relation to fathers, employees,
and employers
EPHESIANS 6:1–9

It is a rare man who succeeds in every area of life and yet remains humble toward his fellow man and toward God. Sir Thomas More was such a man. More was born in London, England in 1478 and died in 1535. He was a man of uncommon character and his example of Christian manhood was so powerful that his legacy endures to this day. He was a faithful husband, father, employee, employer, and Christian.

More came from a well-established family, which provided him an excellent education in secular matters as well as Christian doctrine. Before entering a vigorous law profession, More seriously considered the priesthood. After extensive prayer, study, and counsel, he decided he could not shake the desire to be married. More was married for six years and had four children before his wife died unexpectedly. He married again, choosing a widower named Alice, and they remained happily married until his death.

More's commitment to Christ and his Christian faith was the unwavering compass that charted the course of his life's actions. At the young age of twenty-three, he was elected a member of the English Parliament and immediately began to oppose the king's unjust taxation of the poor, which could have cost him his head if the king saw fit. What spared him was that More always spoke with clear and reasoned arguments and never attacked the person of the king. More was always a faithful subject (employee) of the king, and never sought to undermine his authority, even when he disagreed with him.

As More advanced as a lawyer, his fame grew quickly. He was known to be absolutely fair and just with everyone, rich or poor. This was uncommon in the legal system where bribery and favors for the wealthy and connected were standard practice. More continued to grow in favor with the people and with those in authority, and after various appointments to different political offices, More became Chancellor of England in direct service to King Henry VIII, which was one of the highest offices in the land.

At this time, the Protestant reformation was in full swing and King Henry VIII was seeking a divorce from his first wife, but the pope would not grant him an annulment since his marriage was valid. Emboldened by the Protestant reformers, the king issued a royal proclamation declaring himself head of the Church in England, instead of the pope, and required all priests and bishops to acknowledge him as such. This proclamation would allow the king to grant the false annulment he was seeking. More knew that his office required him to enforce the proclamation, contrary to the Christian faith.

More had unwavering devotion to both his king and his God, and the only way to preserve both was to resign. He immediately lost his income, status, and ability to employ the dozens of servants and housekeepers at his estate in Chelsea. More did not publicly speak out against the king, but because of More's great popularity throughout the country, everyone knew his resignation meant that he disagreed with the king's decision, which did not sit well with the king.

Furthermore, in 1534 the king put forth the Act of Succession, which required one to take an oath swearing acceptance of the king's offspring from his new marriage as legitimate, and that one reject all foreign authority, including the pope. More knew that an oath is a solemn profession before God, and to take an oath that rejects

God's authority (vested in the pope and Church) is to reject God. Therefore, More refused to take the oath.

More always lived his life with heaven as his goal. When he was warned of the grave danger of disagreeing with the king, More replied, "Then, in good faith, between your grace and me is but this, that I shall die today, and you tomorrow." More knew the only thing that truly mattered was his faithfulness to God, because all men eventually die. He knew it served no purpose to reject God and live another day, only to meet death later and find he had rejected God for all eternity.

Upon his refusal to take the oath, Sir Thomas More was immediately imprisoned and eventually convicted on trumped up charges of treason. Due to his firm adherence to Christ and the Church, More was sentenced to death by beheading in 1535. Sir Thomas More was canonized by Pope Pius XI in 1935 and became St. Thomas More. He stands as a model for all men as one who led by example and faithfully served Christ at every stage of his personal life and in all manner of business dealings. Today he is the patron saint of difficult marriages, large families, politicians, and lawyers, and other life situations.

## The Ultimate Role Model

No man can live life in isolation. Every man influences and every man is influenced. The question each one of us must answer is how will we influence others and by whom will we be influenced. We have no choice of whether or not to influence or be influenced, the only choice we have is how this happens. Every time we interact with others in conversation or when we are simply being observed, we have an opportunity to be an influence. Every time we choose to listen or observe someone, we are being influenced. The amount of influence depends on the repetition of the encounters—the greater the repetition, the greater the influence.

Advertising companies know the power of repetition and how it can influence buying habits of the public. If frequent advertising didn't work, businesses would not use it. Successful companies spend millions of dollars to have a famous athlete or actor endorse a product because they know that when men see that guy, they will be drawn to be like him.

Every day, you are a role model to those around you. In essence, you are a living commercial for what you believe. The repetition of your actions will naturally influence those around you, for better or for worse. In the opening story, Thomas More sought to live his life in a manner worthy of emulation, knowing the importance of the positions he held as husband, father, employee, and employer. He knew that Christ was the key to everything and that Jesus related to every aspect of life, not just Sunday morning. Each man must evaluate his commitment to Jesus and decide if he will let Jesus shape every aspect of his life: family, business, pleasure, and so on. You are a role model for those around you. Set an example worthy of emulation. Jesus gave us the great gift of salvation so that we can redeem our minds and actions, helping us achieve the greatest success in this life and getting us to the next

## Man-Pleaser or God-Pleaser | Verses 6–8

**"NOT IN THE WAY OF EYE-SERVICE, AS MEN-PLEASERS, BUT AS SERVANTS OF CHRIST, DOING THE WILL OF GOD FROM THE HEART, RENDERING SERVICE WITH A GOOD WILL AS TO THE LORD AND NOT TO MEN, KNOWING THAT WHATEVER GOOD ANY ONE DOES, HE WILL RECEIVE THE SAME AGAIN FROM THE LORD, WHETHER HE IS A SLAVE OR FREE."**

The general theme of this section is centered on the choice of every man to be either a man-pleaser or God-pleaser.

## Man-Pleaser

To be a man-pleaser means to stick to your religious and moral convictions only insofar as they are acceptable to others. A man-pleaser quickly sheds unpopular beliefs when external pressures become too great. Many choose to be man-pleasers because it is the path of least resistance. For example, you are sitting with a group of guys at lunch and one guy begins to talk in a sexually explicit way about a female co-worker. The other men join in, adding their own suggestive comments. You now have a choice: Will you be an influencer or be influenced? You could jump in and make some salacious contributions. You could laugh along with them and thereby give implicit approval of the conversation. You could stay silent. Or you could speak up and say that the conversation demeans her, and change the subject (in a charitable way of course). Clearly, the most difficult decision would be to speak up, because that could potentially alienate you from the group. A man-pleaser is more concerned with fitting in and looking good than doing what is right.

## God-Pleaser

A God-pleaser, on the other hand, seeks to honor God even if it causes some personal discomfort. Paul says we should do the will of God "from the heart" (Eph 6:6) and not begrudgingly. This can only be done when you truly understand who Jesus is and what He has done for you. Jesus is our source of strength for living the Christian life (Phil 4:12–13; Rom 8:28). As was said earlier, we will only sacrifice for valuable things. Jesus was able to endure the Cross because He understood the purpose of His physical suffering. Jesus explicitly said that He did not seek to please men but to please God (Jn 5:41–44). Paul says that we shouldn't act properly only when others are watching. We should act appropriately at all times because God is always watching. Paul then gives a promise that we will always receive a return on our investment because we cannot out-give God. If we live our life for Him, we will receive blessing in this life and in the life to come (Mt 6:25–34).

## Fathers, Be an Example to Your Children | Verse 4

"FATHERS, DO NOT PROVOKE YOUR CHILDREN TO ANGER, BUT

**BRING THEM UP IN THE DISCIPLINE AND INSTRUCTION OF THE LORD."**

Children are a blessing in many ways. They love to do what we do, to be where we are, and to absorb all that we have the time and patience to give them. In many ways, children end up becoming a mirror of our life, even the unpleasant parts. It is fun to hear our children use our common phrases and mimic our actions, but every now and then our children pick up our bad words and habits. It is amazing to see how much our children learn from us, without ever having to be formally taught. You might find yourself walking through the house and hear one of your children say something he shouldn't. When you call him on it, he replies by saying, "But Daddy, you say that all the time." In that moment you realize the power of your personal example.

Paul specifically addresses the tendency existing in all fathers to provoke their children to anger. Fathers can do this in many ways. We can be too harsh with discipline: You're grounded for a week because you didn't brush your teeth. We can be inconsistent with discipline: One week a child is grounded for not doing a given chore, and the next week there is no consequence. We can also spark anger in our children by speaking too harshly with them, always correcting them, or never giving them a chance just to be kids. Our anger breeds anger in our children.

Paul says the answer is to bring up our children in the discipline and instruction of Jesus. This means we must know Jesus and how He operates for us to be good fathers. As fathers we should lead by example in our spiritual life. The more we get to know Jesus, the more we will see that He is gracious, compassionate, firm, consistent, just, and perfect love. Jesus isn't a doormat, but He brings discipline fitting to the situation and to the person (Mt 21:12–13; Jn 8:1–11). The more you know your Christian faith, the better father you will become.

## Be an Example to Your Boss and Co-Workers | Verses 5–8

**"SLAVES, BE OBEDIENT TO THOSE WHO ARE YOUR EARTHLY**

MASTERS, WITH FEAR AND TREMBLING, IN SINGLENESS OF HEART, AS TO CHRIST; NOT IN THE WAY OF EYE-SERVICE, AS MEN-PLEASERS, BUT AS SERVANTS OF CHRIST, DOING THE WILL OF GOD FROM THE HEART, RENDERING SERVICE WITH A GOOD WILL AS TO THE LORD AND NOT TO MEN, KNOWING THAT WHATEVER GOOD ANY ONE DOES, HE WILL RECEIVE THE SAME AGAIN FROM THE LORD, WHETHER HE IS A SLAVE OR FREE. MASTERS, DO THE SAME TO THEM, AND FORBEAR THREATENING, KNOWING THAT HE WHO IS BOTH THEIR MASTER AND YOURS IS IN HEAVEN, AND THAT THERE IS NO PARTIALITY WITH HIM."

Ever since Adam sinned, our work has been more laborious than it was intended to be (Gen 3:17–19). God intended work to be a joy, but the bottom line is that sometimes work stinks. In this section, Paul is speaking about the relationship between slaves and masters, but it is not too much of a stretch to relate this to employees and employers.

Paul gives us a variation on the theme of wives being subject to husbands as to Christ, and tells men to be obedient to employers (masters) as to Christ. Depending on your employer, this is quite a tall order. You might have one of those loud, insecure, yelling, middle-management type of boss, and the thought of serving him as you would Christ makes your stomach turn.

The point is not to fall on your knees before your boss and kiss his feet, but to recognize that, as a Christian, everything you do is done for Christ. Speaking on this same subject, Paul tells the Church at Colossae, "Whatever your task, work heartily, as serving the Lord and not men, knowing that from the Lord you will receive the inheritance as your reward; you are serving the Lord Christ" (Col 3:23–24).

Your Christian faith should permeate every aspect of your life, including your workplace and business dealings. As an employee, do you show your integrity when writing down your hours worked? Do you pilfer supplies from the office? Do you call in sick when you really are not? When working business deals, do you abide by the law or use unethical loopholes because that's how everyone does business? The question at hand is whether or not your Christian faith is a part of every aspect of your life. Do you live right because of your love for God or only when others are looking? It is often said that a man shows his true character and beliefs when he is alone and no one is watching. Be an example to others and live for Christ at every opportunity in your workplace, especially when no one is watching.

### Be an Example as an Employer

If you are an employer or a manager who oversees employees, you have a great opportunity to influence others in a profound manner. When we talk about God and the workplace, the immediate thought that comes to mind is that many companies forbid direct discussion on religious matters, especially as a boss. Here we can employ the old saying attributed to St. Francis of Assisi, "Preach the gospel at all times, and if necessary use words." One can influence people in many ways without ever having to directly instruct them.

First, Paul says that masters (employers) should "forbear threatening." Forbearance is patient restraint—it takes effort. Employers should not threaten employees, but supervise in a manner that honors the dignity of the person. A manager that tries to get results through coercion and force is not using methods consistent with the Christian life.

Second, Paul reminds us that, before God, both the master and slave are equal. To the Church at Galatia, Paul says of their status before God, "There is neither Jew nor Greek, there is neither slave nor free man, there is neither male nor female; for you are all one in Christ Jesus" (Gal 3:28). We are to treat everyone with equal human dignity because everyone is made in the image and likeness of God (CCC 1700–15).

An employer or manager can live the Gospel in many ways without ever specifically speaking about Christ. Through showing integrity in business decisions, employee appreciation, fairness in decisions, high work ethic, and making it clear that morality is not for sale, an employer can speak very loudly of what he believes. There are small explicit statements of faith you can make, like the

Sign of the Cross and praying before you eat, but if you make those explicit statements and then use foul language, you will only tarnish the name of Christ and the Catholic Church.

God will honor you when you make Him a priority in your life personally and professionally. Employees will respect you when you truly live what you profess to believe and don't give in just to make a good deal or when the pressure is on. If you live in this way, eventually those around you will ask you why you act the way you do, and then you can point them to Jesus.

### Conclusion: Witness First, Speak Second

All men influence those around them; we must make the choice to be an influence for Christ or for Satan. It is important to speak about our Christian faith when called upon, and just as important to consistently live for Christ around family, friends, and co-workers. Pope Paul VI sums up nicely the balance between being one who speaks about the Christian faith and lives the Christian faith, "Modern man listens more willingly to witnesses than to teachers, and if he does listen to teachers, it is because they are witnesses."

St. Thomas More witnessed with his life and became a teacher in a way that far outlived his life. Be an example and a witness to Christ to your children, co-workers, and employees. Live in such a way that will make them want to be like you.

## Study Questions

1. Name three qualities of St. Thomas More that you would like to improve on in your life. Explain.

2. Have you been aware of how much you influence others around you? As you think about it, give an example of how this might be evident.

3. Do you want to be a role model? Why?

4. Have you ever had to choose between pleasing man and pleasing God? In this situation, someone will disapprove—man or God. Whose approval did you seek?

5. Is it more difficult for you to choose holiness when you are alone, when no one is looking? Why?

CHAPTER 11

# Get on Your Knees and Fight Like a Man

How to succeed in your Christian life and in everything else
EPHESIANS 6:10–20

World history is replete with stories of war, one nation trying to conquer another for the purpose of acquiring land, riches, and people. From Alexander the Great in 330 BC to the Fall of Rome in AD 410 to the wars of independence during the eighteenth and nineteenth centuries, mankind seems only to have one method of attack or defense: kill. With the first and second World Wars, the twentieth century showed that the desire to conquer was alive and well. Between ninety million and one hundred million people died as the result of these two wars alone, making them the deadliest wars in history. Although these wars were huge in scale, they were not the only wars of the century. More than two hundred additional wars have been fought between nations.

Is it possible to bring change in a way other than war? Until AD 33, the answer seemed to be no. Prior to that time, only those with swords could advance and conquer, and only those willing to kill could bring change. But at the perfect point in time, a new institution emerged that was able overcome every government and empire without shedding one drop of blood. What appeared in AD 33? The Church. This was not an institution of man's design, but of God's.

Jesus ascended back to heaven in AD 33, leaving Peter and the

Apostles in charge of the Church with the mission to go into all the world and preach the good news of the Gospel of Jesus Christ to every nation—without using force. Jesus foretold the struggles they would endure and said that just as He suffered and was persecuted, so would they. Jesus said the world would hate them because of the Gospel. This proved to be true, as all of the Apostles died as martyrs for Christ except the apostle John.

But the persecution wasn't limited to the Apostles.

First came the persecution of the Roman emperor Nero in AD 64. He was the first to seek widespread persecution of the new Christian Church. But something quite unexpected happened. Instead of the Church being suppressed, it grew. Every act of Christian persecution brought more fervent prayer and a more vigorous proclamation of the Gospel.

The second century saw more persecutions from Rome and the surrounding regions, and yet again, the threat of death did not diminish the Church. St. Justin writes around AD 160, "It is plain that, though beheaded, and crucified, and thrown to wild beasts, and chains, and fire, and all other kinds of torture, we do not give up our confession; but, the more such things happen, the more others in larger numbers become faithful." As before, the Church continued to pray and proclaim.

Christians would suffer persecution on and off for the next 143 years, until the reign of the Roman emperor Diocletian. In AD 303, he unleashed a campaign against the whole of Christianity like never before seen. Thousands upon thousands were killed for professing Christ, but as Tertullian had said about one hundred years earlier, "The blood of the martyrs is the seed of the Church." The more Diocletian advanced with the sword, the more another sword became stronger: the sword of the spirit, the Word of God. The more he killed, the more the Church prayed and waged spiritual warfare. The words of St. Paul rang in the ears of the Church, "We are not contending against flesh and blood, but against the principalities, against the powers . . . against the spiritual hosts of wickedness in the heavenly places" (Eph 6:12). Even though the aggressor was physical, the Church knew the source of the threat was spiritual.

The next emperor was Constantine. Before advancing into battle, Constantine had a vision of a cross with the Chi and Rho (signifying Christ), and the inscription "Under this sign you shall conquer." Constantine attributed his military victory to divine help and subsequently issued the Edict of Toleration, which formally ended the legal killing of Christians. Without one sword, without one battle, without shedding one drop of blood, the Church overcame the Roman Empire. Thus ended 249 years of Christian persecution from Nero to Constantine.

From that point on, the Church has endeavored to fulfill Jesus' command to go into all the world and preach the good news of the Gospel. The Church has successfully entered nearly every nation with missionaries and it has never advanced the Gospel through violence. (The crusades and inquisitions were not efforts to advance the Gospel. They had very different goals than evangelistic missions.) The Christian Church is the oldest, largest institution of its kind. No war, no failing government, no persecution could ever cause it to cease because it is not of man's design, but God's. The power of prayer and the Word of God are able to accomplish what no sword ever could.

## The Strength that Never Fades | Verse 10

**"FINALLY, BE STRONG IN THE LORD AND IN THE STRENGTH OF HIS MIGHT."**

We finally arrive at the end of Paul's instruction for us. As a master craftsman, Paul has systematically laid out what is needed to understand our Christian faith and to live it. Paul helped us see who Jesus is, what He has done for us, and what our response is to be toward Him and toward our fellow man. Like most men, you might feel that the bar has been set too high. You might feel like you cannot actually do what has been asked of you. If this is how you feel, you are a wise man. You don't have what it takes in your humanity alone. Namely, you can't accomplish God's plan with only human strength.

You must accomplish God's plan with God's strength. Thankfully, Paul ends his letter to the Ephesians with step-by-step instructions on how to succeed in the Christian life, which means succeeding in every area of life because Christ is the key to everything. Paul has saved the best for last.

Paul begins this last section with an exhortation for us to be strong in the strength of the Lord. All men like to think they are physically strong, and some actually are, but even if you are the strongest man in the world, your strength will eventually fade. God provides an unlimited source of strength for men, but we do not receive this power through physical methods like bench presses, squats, or energy drinks. We receive God's strength through spiritual exercises, and this strength can *never* be taken away by someone else. It can only be forfeited by us. We begin to receive God's strength as we grow in understanding the Christian faith, but we must transition to active spiritual conditioning if we hope to live the high calling of the Gospel. This conditioning is what Paul outlines in this final section.

## Identifying the Enemy | Verse 12

**"FOR WE ARE NOT CONTENDING AGAINST FLESH AND BLOOD, BUT AGAINST THE PRINCIPALITIES, AGAINST THE POWERS, AGAINST THE WORLD RULERS OF THIS PRESENT DARKNESS, AGAINST THE SPIRITUAL HOSTS OF WICKEDNESS IN THE HEAVENLY PLACES."**

Why must we actively pursue spiritual conditioning? Because we are actively being pursued by a real enemy. Who is the enemy? Paul tells us in the previous verse that the enemy is the devil, Satan. Paul goes on in verse twelve to list different levels of the demonic realm. While it is not as important to know specifics about these demonic leaders, it is important to know that there is a real spiritual realm with real demonic forces, who really want to destroy your relationship with God and therefore your eternal soul. Satan is not a myth (CCC 391–95, 2850–54).

The enemy is spiritual and not physical, but he does manifest himself physically. Satan will use any medium to draw you and your family away from each other and from God: TV, movies, internet, music, video games, food, alcohol, drugs, pornography, magazines, other women, other men, your thoughts, career, cars, and just about anything else. Everything in this list, except illegal drugs and pornography, are not objectively sinful. They only become sinful when used in a manner contrary to truth. For example, the internet is not sinful, but using the internet to find porn is sinful.

Once you understand who the enemy is and how he operates, isolate the threats in your life and take them out. Don't mess around with Satan. He is coming to attack you and your family. St. Peter tells us in his first letter, "Be sober, be watchful. Your adversary the devil prowls around like a roaring lion, seeking some one to devour" (1 Pet 5:8). Satan would like nothing more than to devour you through the sins of this world. While we must isolate the physical threats of our spiritual enemy, we must never conclude that we are to hate people. Our quarrel is with Satan. He is the object of our disdain (CCC 2851). We should always seek to love people and pray for them. Thankfully, we do not need to fear Satan. Jesus has already won the victory. All we need to do is make use of the victory already won through Christ.[1]

## Get Dressed for Battle and Stand Your Ground | Verses 11, 13

**"PUT ON THE WHOLE ARMOR OF GOD, THAT YOU MAY BE ABLE TO STAND AGAINST THE WILES OF THE DEVIL. . . . THEREFORE TAKE THE WHOLE ARMOR OF GOD, THAT YOU MAY BE ABLE TO WITHSTAND IN THE EVIL DAY, AND HAVING DONE ALL, TO STAND."**

No soldier would show up to battle without proper weapons and clothing, nor would he show up with only half of what he needs. With this in mind Paul says, "Put on the whole armor of God." Step one in growing in the strength of God is to get completely dressed for battle, to put on the *whole* armor. Too many men are trying to live the Christian life half dressed. You've protected your chest, but

---

1. CCC 2853; 1 Cor 15:57; Jn 14:30; Rom 8:37; Col 2:13–15; Heb 2:14; 1 Jn 5:4.

left your head exposed. You've got a shield, but no sword. God has given you everything you need to succeed in the Christian life, but the greatest sword in the world does you no good if it stays in closet.

With this spiritual armor you can *stand* against the attacks of the devil. Standing is a sign of strength and defiance. The traditional rules of boxing have held that as long as a fighter can get to his feet he is allowed to fight. The sign of defeat is being unable stand. In long spiritual battles, it can become difficult to swing your sword or raise your shield. Sometimes all you can do is stand. As if to anticipate the battles we will endure, Paul says that after you have done all you can do, to simply stand. Every time you choose Christ instead of sin, you stand against the devil.

Defy the attack of Satan and stand. Even if you are tired, stand. Put your arm around the guy next to you, raise each other up, and stand. In the words of Rocky Balboa, "It ain't how hard you hit; it's about how hard you can get hit, and keep moving forward."[2] Satan is going to throw everything he can at you, and when you remain standing, you defy him. The key to being able to stand is to get fully dressed for battle, to put on the whole armor of God.

## Strong Defense and Focused Offense

If we are going to fight a spiritual enemy, we need spiritual armor and weapons. You can't conquer a spiritual condition like sin with a physical sword. That's the wrong weapon for the job. Paul describes six pieces of the armor of God, each designed for a specific purpose. The first five are defensive and the sixth is offensive.

## Belt of Truth

Our culture presents lies as if they are truth. For example, we are told that money, sex, and power will fulfill us; divorce will bring

2. *Rocky Balboa.* Directed by Sylvester Stallone (Hollywood: Metro-Goldwyn-Mayer, 2006).

peace; abortion is not murder. These lies come at us through every possible medium. If we want to stand against the devil and find true fulfillment, we must be grounded in real truth.

What is truth? The better question is: Who is truth? Jesus is the truth. Jesus said, "I am the way, and the truth, and the life; no one comes to the Father, but by me" (Jn 14:6). Jesus didn't say He knows where to find the way, the truth, and the life, but that He *is* the way, the truth, and the life. The more you know Jesus, the more you will know the truth and the truth will set you free (Jn 8:31, 32, 36). The clearest succinct truth about Jesus is found in the Bible. Read it daily. Put on your belt daily. The belt is the centerpiece of the armor and holds the sheath for your sword; it holds your pants up and supports your breastplate as well. Without your belt, your entire armor comes apart. Truth—don't leave home without it.

## Breastplate of Righteousness

Next to your head, your chest houses the most important organs in your body and it is the easiest target. Your heart and lungs are exposed without your breastplate. If you are not protected by righteousness, your heart will be drawn away to unrighteousness and you will find yourself gasping for breath. All sin is unrighteousness, but righteousness is found in Jesus Christ (1 Cor 1:30; 1 Pet 3:18; 2 Pet 1:1). St. John says, "I am writing this to you so that you may not sin; but if any one does sin, we have an advocate with the Father, Jesus Christ the righteous" (1 Jn 2:1). The more you get to know Jesus Christ, the more your heart will be safeguarded from the ravages of sin and you will breathe deep the peace of God.

## Shoes of the Gospel of Peace

Your feet are what get you from one place to another. If your feet are shot, you have no hope of getting away from the enemy. Your shoes protect your feet and allow you to be mobile and nimble. What is key to keeping you mobile so you can flee from, or attack, the enemy? The Gospel of Jesus Christ, which is a gospel of peace (see chapter four). What is the Gospel? The word "gospel" literally means "good news." The Gospel is the good news: Out of love, Jesus came to save sinners by conquering sin and death through His sacrifice on the Cross and Resurrection from the grave. Through faith in Jesus, by grace, we can be restored to God, overcome sin, and live fulfilled lives on earth and forever in heaven. Ultimately the good news is Jesus. The more you get to know Jesus, the more your feet are prepared for battle.

## Shield of Faith

Your shield is the most active of your defenses. Your shield can move to the location of the threat—above, left, right, or front. Paul makes the gravity of the attack clear by saying that the enemy will launch flaming arrows (darts) at us. Arrows are bad enough, but flaming arrows are much worse and can cause great damage. Paul says your shield doesn't just block the arrows, but it puts out the fire as well. What is your shield? Faith. The writer of Hebrews says, "Without faith it is impossible to please him [God]. For whoever would draw near to God must believe that he exists and that he rewards those who seek him" (11:6). True Christian faith is not just an intellectual belief in the existence of God (Jas 2:18–20), but it is a living faith in Jesus Christ that comes to life through love-filled action (Gal 5:6; 1 Cor 13:1–3, 13). Faith is that which allows us to believe in what we cannot yet see. Again, Hebrews says, "Faith is the assurance of things hoped for, the conviction of things not seen" (11:1). Faith is not blind, but is rooted in hope, the confident expectation of salvation in Jesus Christ. The object of our faith is Jesus. The more you get to know Jesus, the stronger your faith will become and the more you will be able to extinguish the enemy's flaming arrows of lies.

## Helmet of Salvation

Your body can endure many wounds and still survive, but if your head takes a direct hit, your chances of survival are greatly diminished. Paul says to put on the helmet of salvation. Just as the brain is the source of all the body's actions, our salvation in Jesus Christ is the source of our ability to wage this spiritual war. Paul challenges us in Romans to "not be conformed to this world but be transformed by the renewal of your mind." (Rom 12:2; see also Eph 4:23). If your mind is good, you can control your entire body. If you are firmly rooted in your salvation, the saving work of Jesus Christ, your spiritual actions will follow your well-formed mind. The more you understand who Jesus is and what He has done, the more your mind is protected, renewed, and grounded in truth.

## Sword of the Spirit

At last, we have our offensive weapon—the sword. While our defensive armor enables us to stand against the devil, the sword enables us to defeat Satan. As with the rest of the armor, the sword is not rooted in us, but in Jesus Christ, *the* Word of God (Jn 1:1–14). While Jesus is specifically and personally the Word of God, the Scriptures are also the Word of God in written form, inspired by the Holy Spirit.[3] When you know Scripture, you have access to a powerful offensive weapon that can defeat Satan. When Jesus was tempted three times in the desert by Satan, three times He defeated Satan by saying, "It is written . . ." and quoting the truth of the Word of God found in Scripture (Mt 4:1–11). Hebrews says, "The word of God is living and active, sharper than any two-edged sword, piercing to the division of soul and spirit, of joints and marrow, and discerning the thoughts and intentions of the heart" (4:12). The Word of God in Scripture is powerful because it is Jesus speaking. The more you get to know the Bible, the more you will know Jesus, the Word of

---

3. Sacred Tradition and Sacred Scripture make one deposit of the Word of God; CCC 81, 104; 2 Tim 3:16.

God, and will be able to wield a powerful weapon against the enemy. Has Satan made inroads into your life? Get out your sword! Is Satan harassing your family? Use your sword! Is Satan tracking your children? Swing your sword and strike him a deadly blow.

## The Power of Prayer

Finally, and most importantly, Paul says to pray. While you are to stand against the devil, you are to get on your knees before God. The greatest battles are waged on our knees before God in prayer. A real man knows how to fight on his knees. How often should you pray? Paul says to pray always! Whenever you can, offer up a prayer to God. When you are tempted, pray. When you are happy, pray. When life is good or bad, pray. Never stop praying. Paul says to pray in the Spirit, which means to allow your prayer to be Spirit led. Don't let your prayer be mechanical and mindless, but ask the Holy Spirit for direction so that you can pray effectively. Praying a memorized prayer like the Rosary doesn't have to be mechanical if the intentions offered up are Spirit led and your reflections on the mysteries are Spirit led. Our prayer time with God is when we are spiritually replenished. If you only fight, and never pray, you will wear out. If you fight and pray, you will wage spiritual warfare with God's strength that will never fade. Also, don't forget that the Mass is the most powerful prayer of the Church. When you go to Mass, you are entering into an hour-long prayer. Make sure to take the time to properly prepare yourself and your family for Mass so that it will be as fruitful as possible.

## Conclusion

Satan is real and he is trying to snatch you (and your family) into hell, and to do so he is manifesting himself through every nook and cranny in our culture. The good news is that Satan is no match for Jesus. When you battle Satan with the power of Jesus, you successfully run him out of your life. The key is to stop fighting this spiritual battle with only half your armor. Put on the whole armor of God.

As we've clearly seen, every piece of spiritual armor has to do with Jesus Christ. Christ is the key to everything. Get dressed for battle and give God a chance to change the unchangeable, as did the early Church. Is your marriage struggling? Jesus can restore you. Are your children struggling? Jesus can restore them. Does your mind stray to the unholy? Jesus can restore it. Nothing is impossible for God! (Mk 9:23). He can overcome foul language, alcohol and tobacco addictions, anger problems, broken marriages, sexual addictions, materialism, and every other vice Satan uses to keep us from being all that God desires us to be. The battle is spiritual, and when you use the spiritual tools to fight this battle, you will find victory over things that never seemed possible.

## Study Questions

1. Do you feel the spiritual bar has been set too high? Do you feel you cannot do and be what God is asking of you? Explain.

2. Have you ever entered into a program of strong, physical conditioning? Did it pay off?

3. To be strong in faith, you need to actively pursue *spiritual* conditioning because the enemy actively pursues you. How are you doing this? Do you realize Satan is not a myth?

4. What specific things in your life does Satan use to draw you away from your spiritual training?

5. Has the devil ever hit you so hard you weren't sure you could ever stand back up? Which part of the armor came to your rescue?

# CHAPTER 12

# Finish Well

Fix your eyes on Jesus and run the race together
EPHESIANS 6:21–23

Finishing well is the final goal of any journey, and our Christian life is no different. Paul has presented us with an excellent training regimen, and now it is our job to use what he provided and run the race: the Christian life. Through faith and Baptism we began this race. Through hope and love we must persevere in the race until the very end.

In the 1981 movie *Chariots of Fire*, running coach Sam Mussabini prepares Harold Abrahams for the 1924 Olympics. Mussabini begins by showing Abrahams images of his competitors and describing their strengths and weaknesses. He shows a slide of a hundred-meter race between Charlie Paddock and Jackson Scholz. Scholz, who was called the "New York Thunderbolt," had what it took to beat Paddock. Mussabini explains that Scholz had the race won, but in the last moments he took his eyes off the finish line and turned his head right to look at his opponent. The look cost him the race. As Scholz looked right, Paddock leaned forward and won.

Scholz took his eyes off of the finish. He stopped focusing on the final goal and instead focused on the things around him. Scholz had what it took to win, but in the end, he let up and lost. It bears repeating: The Christian life must be lived through God's strength, but we must fix our minds on finishing well. We must commit to run the race to the end. In fact, comparing the Christian life to running a race is one of Paul's favorite analogies.

### Run with Perseverance

Paul was very aware that he, too, must finish well. Just because he was an Apostle commissioned by Jesus did not mean he was free from keeping his eye on the finish line and finishing well. He says to the Corinthian church,

> Do you not know that in a race all the runners compete, but only one receives the prize? So run that you may obtain it. Every athlete exercises self-control in all things. They do it to receive a perishable wreath, but we an imperishable. Well, I do not run aimlessly, I do not box as one beating the air; but I pommel my body and subdue it, lest after preaching to others I myself should be disqualified. (1 Cor 9:24–27)

Paul, toward the end of his life, declares he has successfully reached the end. He says to his young disciple Timothy, "For I am already on the point of being sacrificed; the time of my departure has come. I have fought the good fight, I have finished the race, I have kept the faith" (2 Tim 4:6–7). Each man must make his own decision to run the race. No one can make this decision for you. Paul, the likely author of Hebrews, invites us to run the race in light of the great gift of salvation made available through Jesus Christ. He invites us to persevere, keeping our eyes on Jesus, while giving us some perspective that our struggle against sin has not been so great that we have had to shed blood (like the martyrs Polycarp, Thomas More, and the thousands of others since the Church began). Paul says,

Therefore, since we are surrounded by so great

a cloud of witnesses, let us also lay aside every weight, and sin which clings so closely, and let us run with perseverance the race that is set before us, looking to Jesus the pioneer and perfecter of our faith, who for the joy that was set before him endured the cross, despising the shame, and is seated at the right hand of the throne of God. Consider him who endured from sinners such hostility against himself, so that you may not grow weary or fainthearted. In your struggle against sin you have not yet resisted to the point of shedding your blood. (Heb 12:1–4)

This is a great call to every man: lay aside every sin which clings so closely, and run the race set before you with perseverance. Don't turn your head to the right or to the left. Keep your eyes on Jesus. By grace, Jesus brought faith alive in you and He is the one who will see you through to the end.

## Don't Run Alone | Verses 21-22

There are many Lone Ranger-type stories where one man goes in and saves the day against all odds, but that is not how real life works. God didn't call you to be a spiritual Rambo, but to be part of a team called the Church. You can't play football with one man on the field, and neither can you live the Christian life on your own. You need your fellow brothers in Christ and your brothers in Christ need you. Through the power of God, you can stand together against Satan. If you are divided, you make for easy picking.

Paul is very aware of the need for fraternal support, and in these closing verses he announces the sending of Tychicus (pronounced Tÿch' ĭcus) to the Church at Ephesus. Tychicus will give them an update on Paul's condition and bring encouragement to the young Church. As men, we need to foster this kind of fraternal bond. It is important for us to know how each other is doing and to encourage one another. At different times some men will be stronger than others, and like any good team, when needed, different players will bear more of the load to help the others succeed. When we come together to support one another we take one step closer to the finish line.

## The Invitation

At the beginning of this study you were invited to discover (or grow deeper in) the truest meaning of life and a power and authority that will stay with you no matter what circumstances life brings (see Introduction). Like Paul, who was knocked off his horse through an encounter with Jesus, you were invited to set aside the perceived authority and security of earthly attachments, and embrace Jesus to find the life truly worth living. When Jesus takes the lead, you find success and satisfaction in the essentials of life: marriage, family, business, sexuality, money, friendships, and most importantly, getting to heaven.

There is vulnerability in letting Jesus take the lead, but what you receive in return is the unshakable security of knowing who you are, who God is, and what He expects of you. When you allow Jesus to truly *be* Lord of your life, you set aside worldly things with their perception of value in exchange for the riches of Christ. Let us take a brief look at where we have been throughout this study.

> Sonship: As a Christian, you are a son of God and a full heir to His kingdom.
> Understanding: Comprehending the Christian faith is the key to living it—invest for the long-term.
> Grace: Even though you were dead in sin, Jesus made you alive through the Cross.
> Peace: Through Jesus you can have peace with God and with all men.
> Church: Through the Church, God has been personally searching for you.

> Consistency: If we say we believe in Jesus, we should live for Jesus.
> Effectiveness: Through Jesus we can replace wasted efforts with life changing action.
> Imitation: We are to follow the example of Jesus in our actions.
> Sacrifice: Men are divinely created to serve and protect and lead our wives through sacrifice.
> Role Models: We should be role models to all who observe us, especially our children.
> Prayer: Spiritual warfare is real and we must get dressed for battle and fight on our knees.
> Victory: Don't stop until you cross the finish line.

This trip through Ephesians is just the beginning. There's no way you would be expected to master the Christian life after reading a few chapters of the Bible, but every journey begins with one step. The key to running this race is remembering it is a marathon and not a sprint. You must pace yourself, run with wisdom, and realize that you can't change everything overnight. While it is a marathon, none of us know when our earthly lives will end. It could end today, tomorrow, next week, or fifty years from now. So don't start the race tomorrow or an hour from now. "Behold, now is the acceptable time; behold now is the day of salvation" (2 Cor 6:2). When Jesus called the Apostles, immediately they followed Him, immediately they left their nets and their tax tables.

## Pacing Yourself

So how do you set a good pace for this race? There are a number of practical things you can do, one of which is recognizing that Christ gave us the seven sacraments to be tangible points of contact with Him. The sacraments are not just things we do because we're Catholic, but are powerful encounters with Christ if we are prepared to meet Him. The two sacraments available for frequent use are the Sacrament of Penance (Confession) and the Mass (Eucharist).

## Sacrament of Penance

Make frequent use of the Sacrament of Penance, especially if you are trying to overcome pervasive sin. Satan knows we will be ineffective if we are afraid to confess our sin. We think that when our sin is hidden, people will accept us more, but that is a tactic of the prowling lion, Satan. Come to Jesus humbly, but confident in the Sacrament of Penance (Heb 10:16–22), knowing He *always* forgives you when you truly repent. You don't have to wonder whether Jesus will forgive you. When you genuinely confess, you are always forgiven.

## Mass

Christ gave us the Mass so that we would be nourished in two ways: through the Scriptures, the written Word of God, and through the Eucharist, the Word of God made flesh.[1] The Mass is our supreme act of worship toward God—where we worship in spirit and in truth (Jn 4:23–24). To get the most out of Mass, you must come ready to receive. If you get up late, rush around, yell at the kids, and walk in during the readings, it's a good bet you won't get much out of Mass. But if you do small things to prepare yourself and your family, like reading through the Scriptures for the day while at home (and discuss them) and showing up ten minutes early so you can pray, you'll find yourself getting more out of Mass than you previously have.

## Bible

In addition to the sacraments, regular Bible reading is essential to the Christian life. The Church specifically says that all the Christian faithful should learn about the "excellent knowledge of Jesus Christ" (Phil 3:8) through "frequent reading of the divine Scriptures" (CCC

---

1. CCC 1346–1347; these two aspects are also seen on the road to Emmaus in Lk 24:13–35.

133) and that "ignorance of the Scriptures is ignorance of Christ" (*Dei Verbum*, 25; CCC 133). The more you know the written word of God, the stronger your sword of the Spirit becomes.

## Prayer

We are fighting a spiritual battle in the Christian life and prayer is the primary way we fight. If you're like most men, you struggle to have a regular prayer time or have never set aside a regular time for prayer. As a start, make sure to pray at the simple times, like before meals and with your children before bed. Make prayer a part of the daily routine. Become comfortable praying with your own words as well as with memorized prayers. As you have opportunity, pray at least one decade of the Rosary and more if you have time. Clearly tell God your intentions so that your requests will be made known to Him (Phil 4:6). Lastly, reclaim dead time, like driving in the car. Driving is a great time to turn off the radio and talk to God.

## Fellowship

Finally, there is nothing like genuine Christian fellowship to help you endure throughout the race. From time to time everyone struggles, and when we run together we have a much greater chance at success. Find time to get together with other men, families, and people of like mind. If there's nothing at your parish, get your pastor's permission and start something. The early Church was founded with a profound sense of community and fellowship (CCC 949–53), and without this it would not have survived.

## Till Death Do Us Part

Paul's last words in his Letter to the Ephesians are, "Grace be with all who love our Lord Jesus Christ with love undying." May it be said of each one of us that our love for God remained until our death. There is a lot of life to be lived between now and our death, and none of us knows exactly what he will do when faced with a challenge, but we can prepare now for the challenges ahead. Like the soldier that endures rigorous training to prepare to meet the enemy, regardless of the battlefield, may we spiritually prepare now so that we will be ready to stand against Satan, regardless of the attack.

Succeeding in the Christian life does not happen by accident, but intentionally. Don't look to the left or right, but keep your eyes fixed on Jesus who stands at the finish line. Finish well. And to every man who seeks a life worth living in Christ, "peace be to the brethren, and love with faith, from God the Father and the Lord Jesus Christ."

## Study Questions

1. If the Christian life is a race with a finish line, what is the prize?

2. What might be one of the weights you want to lay aside so you can run freely and well?

3. To finish the race means to keep the faith until the end of your life. Have you made that commitment?

4. Where in your life do you find your greatest support and encouragement?

5. When you think of letting Jesus take the lead in every area, do you feel safe or vulnerable?